POEMS

OF

WILLIAM BLAKE

POEMS

OF

WILLIAM BLAKE

EDITED BY

W. B. YEATS

ROUTLEDGE & KEGAN PAUL
LONDON, BOSTON, MELBOURNE AND HENLEY

First published in 1905
by George Routledge & Sons Ltd.
Fourth impression published 1969
by Routledge & Kegan Paul Plc.
39 Store Street, London WC1E 7DD
9 Park Street, Boston, Mass. 02108, U.S.A.
296 Beaconsfield Parade, Middle Park,
Melbourne, 3206, Australia, and
Broadway House, Newtown Road,
Henley-on-Thames,
Oxon RG9 1EN
Reprinted and first published as a
paperback in 1979
Reprinted in 1983 by
The Thetford Press Ltd., Thetford, Norfolk

ISBN 0 7100 0174 6 (p)

CONTENTS

SONGS OF EXPERIENCE

IDEAS OF GOOD AND EVIL

INTRODUCTION

INTRODUCTION

EARLY in the eighteenth century a certain John O'Neil got into debt and difficulties, these latter apparently political to some extent ; and escaped both by marrying a woman named Ellen Blake, who kept a shebeen at Rathmines, Dublin, and taking her name. He had a son James, I am told, by a previous wife or mistress, and this son took also the name of Blake, and in due course married, settled in London as a hosier, and became the father of five children, one of whom was the subject of this memoir. John O'Neil had also a son by his wife Ellen ; and this son, settling in Malaga, in Spain, entered the wine trade, and became the founder of a family, and from one of this family, Dr. Carter Blake, I have the story. James Blake was living over his shop at 28, Broad Street, Golden Square, when, in the year 1757, his son William Blake was born. He had already a son John, the best beloved of father and mother, who grew up to be the black sheep of the family, and he begot afterwards James, who was to pester William with what Tatham calls " bread and cheese advice ", and Robert, whom William came to love like his own soul, and a daughter, of whom we hear little, and among that little not

even her name.   This family grew up among
ideas less conventional than might be looked
for in the house of a small shopkeeper.
Swedenborgianism was then creeping into
England, and the hosier's shop was one of
the places where it had found shelter.
The prophecies and visions of the new
illumination were doubtless a very common
subject of talk about the tea-table at night,
and must have found ready welcome from
William Blake.   One prophecy certainly
did sink into his mind.   Swedenborg had
said that the old world ended, and the new
began, in the year 1757.   From that day
forward the old theologies were rolled up
like a scroll, and the new Jerusalem came
upon the earth.   How often this prophecy
concerning the year of his birth may have
rung in the ears of William Blake we know
not ; but certainly it could hardly have
done other than ring there, when his strange
gift began to develop and fill the darkness
with shadowy faces and the green meadows
with phantom footsteps.   He must often
have thought that so strange a faculty may
well have come not wholly unannounced,
that it was the first glimmer of the great
new illumination.   In later life he called
the seeing of visions being in Eden ; and
in his system Eden came again when the old
theology passed away.   The profound sanity
of his inspiration is proved by his never
having, no matter how great the contrast

between himself and the blind men and women about him, pronounced himself to be chosen and set apart alone among men. Wiser than Swedenborg, he saw that he had but what all men might have if they would, and that God spoke through him but as He had spoken through the great men of all ages and countries. The first vision we have record of looks strange enough through the clouded glass of Crab Robinson's diary. "God put his forehead to the window"; and Blake, being but four years old, set up a scream. Another authority tells how he strayed later on into the fields at Peckham Rye, and passed a tree full of angels, their bright wings shining among the boughs. There is record, too, of his finding Ezekiel sitting one summer day in the open fields, and of his being beaten by his mother for bringing home so unlikely a story.

His preparation for his great calling went on all the more smoothly in that he was never sent to school. He began early to prove his aphorism, "The tigers of wrath are wiser than the horses of instruction," and to govern his life by thought and impulse alone. His father noticing how ill he brooked any kind of authority, and to what great anger he was moved by a blow, resolved to spare him the contest that must needs have arisen between his passionate mood and the narrow pedagogy of the time. He left him to steer his course unaided, and the boy made excellent use of this freedom, reading all that came to hand, poring over Swedenborg, and even, it has been surmised, dipping into profound Boehme, then coming out in translation under the editorship of William Law. Paracelsus, a hero of Blake's later days, has written that " he who would know the book of Nature must walk with his feet upon its leaves." Blake began early to fulfil the saying, and to bridge over the gaps in his reading with meditations in the country lanes, and to store his memory with the country sights and sounds that shine and murmur through all his verse. The sulphurous tide of London brick and stone had not then submerged all pleasant walks and kindly solitudes ; for a little to the north of Golden Square, and almost abutting upon Oxford Street, were "the fields of cows by Wellings' Farm " ; and away westward, at Bayswater, were willow-bordered brooks, where perhaps a stray kingfisher might still be found ; and but little to the south, spread far and wide the green lanes and shadowy boscage of Surrey. He had ever close at hand the two things most needed for noble meditation—multitude and solitude.

His father, seeing the imaginative bent of his mind, resolved to make a painter of him ; but the boy, hearing how great a premium must be paid for his apprenticeship, said it would be unfair to his brothers and sister, and asked to be set to engraving instead. Accordingly, after three or four years' study at the drawing-school of a certain Parr, whose house stood where now King William Street joins the Strand, we find him working with an engraver called Basire. Basire was an excellent engraver, but belonged to a school then giving way before more graceful if less austere methods. His influence never forsook Blake, who always preserved an enthusiastic remembrance of him and his methods. He was not the master first selected. Blake had been brought to the studio of one Rylands, then at the summit of popularity, but had said, "Father, I do not like the man's look; he looks as if he would live to be hanged"—a prophecy that was fulfilled twelve years later, when Rylands was hanged for forgery.

Blake worked two years at Basire's house, 31, Great Queen Street (now a carriage-builder's) and just opposite the *Freemason's Tavern*. Then some trouble arose among the apprentices, and Basire thought best to send him from amongst them. One authority, Malkin, says he did so because Blake "declined to take part with his master against his fellow-apprentices", and that Basire declared him to be "too simple and they too cunning";

while another authority, Tatham, who probably had his information from Mrs. Blake, sets it down to " matters of intellectual argument " between Blake and his fellows, which sounds likely enough, and rejoices greatly in the change, for, " had things gone otherwise, he might never have been more than a mere engraver." Both causes may have weighed with Basire, and certainly it is well for Blake that the change came, though we may doubt if his insurgent will and obstinate heart would ever, despite Tatham, have let him rest content to be a mere inscriber on steel or copper of other men's imaginings, whether " things had gone otherwise " or no. He was packed off to Westminster Abbey to draw the monuments, pillars, and the like, and was kept there five years. At first he was greatly annoyed by the Westminster students, who had then the right to stray about the Abbey as they would. The man or boy of genius is very generally hated or scorned by the average man or boy until the day come for him to charm them into unwilling homage. Until that day he has often to cry with Blake, " Why was I not born with a different face ? " for his abstracted ways and his strange interests arouse that hatred of the uncommon which lies deep in the common heart. It is said that if you tie a piece of red cloth to a gull's leg its fellow-gulls will

peck it to death. Shelley, tormented by
the gull-like animosity of his schoolfellows,
plunged a pen through the hand of a tor-
mentor. Blake leant out from a scaffolding
where he sat at work and flung a West-
minster student from a cornice, whither he
had climbed the better to tease him. The
boy fell heavily upon the stone floor, and
Blake went off and laid a formal complaint
before the Dean. " The tigers of wrath "
vindicated their wisdom, for the students
were ever after shut out of the Abbey.
Blake knew well how to temper anger
with prudence and make it a harmless
and obedient servant. It has been told of
him that he once grew angry with a plate
he was engraving, and flung it across the
room. " Did you not injure it ? " asked
some one afterwards. " I took good care
of that ", was the reply. Then, too, we
have his own aphorism—

> " To be in a passion you good may do,
>   But no good if a passion is in you."

No matter how enthusiastically he com-
mended enthusiasm, alike of love and of
hate, he ever intended the mind to be master
over all. He explicitly condemns, likewise,
all anger aimed against persons instead of
states of mind, though his own practice
sometimes but ill conformed to his precept.
He, however, held any enthusiastic hatred
to be better than the mildness founded upon
unbelief and cowardice, for it was his firm

conviction that the cold, logical, analytic
faculty was the most murderous of all.
It was necessary even for the unwise man to
grow fierce in the defence of falsehood,
" that enthusiasm and life may not cease."
He is unlikely to have thought out these
matters in detail in the early days we write
of ; but few men have ever mirrored their
temperament in their philosophy as clearly
as he did, and to his philosophy, accordingly,
we must turn again and again.

If Blake learned Nature in his long
rambles southward in Surrey, and up
northward by Wellings' Farm, he learned
to know Art among the tombs and pointed
ceilings of the Abbey. Its towers and
spire are hieroglyphs for poetic inspiration
in more than one of his later drawings.
" Gothic form ", he was wont to write,
" is living form " ; and the shadows of the
great Abbey may well have been the shelter
that preserved him from the pseudo-classical
ideas of his time. In some lines added at a
later date to an engraving made now, he
compares the great Gothic churches to the
tomb of Christ. Christ was his symbolic
name for the imagination, and the tomb of
Christ could be no other than a shelter,
where imagination might sleep in peace
until the hour of God should awaken it.
What more beautiful shelter could he have
found than this ancient Abbey ? Outside
the " indefinite " multitude brawled and

pushed, and inside the " definite " forms of
art and vision congregated, and were at
peace.

One day certain shapes, purporting to
be the twelve Apostles, gathered about the
altar ; and doubtless many another vision
appeared likewise, though he probably did
not yet begin to think much about their
meaning and their message. He was now
busy with *Edward III* and other histori-
cal fragments, and may have caught some-
thing of his historical enthusiasm from the
monuments about him. Another inspiration
came to him in the works of Chatterton,
who, five years his elder, had lately published
the poems of " T. Rowlie." The " Bard's
Song ", at the end of *Edward III* shows
the influence of the " English metamor-
phosis " very visibly. He must also have
read Spenser and the Elizabethan drama-
tists. This was the only purely literary
and purely artistic period of his life ; for
in a very short time he came to look upon
poetry and art as a language for the utter-
ance of conceptions, which, however beauti-
ful, were none the less thought out more
for their visionary truth than for their beauty.
The change made him a greater poet and a
greater artist ; for " He that findeth his
life shall lose it, and he that loseth his life
for My sake shall find it."

In his twentieth year his apprenticeship
came to an end, and he began engraving

and drawing upon his own account. Now
too, he made the acquaintance of Flaxman
and Fuseli, who became his life-long friends,
despite one short interruption in the case
of the first, brought about by a sudden
descent of " the tigers of wrath." At this
time also he began courting one Polly or
Clara Woods, " a lovely little girl ", who took
walks with him here and there, and then
whistled him down the wind. Many of his
descriptions of " Vala " and other symbolic
women, and some few of the illustrations
to the " Prophetic Books ", such as the false,
smiling face at the bottom of one of the
pages of " Vala " (see *The · Works of
William Blake*, page 5 of the lithographs
from " Vala "), and more than one of the
lyrics, such as " Love's Secret ", may con-
ceivably owe their inspiration to her. In-
dubitably a certain type of feminine beauty,
at once soft and cruel, emotional and egotis-
tic, filled Blake with a mingled terror and
wonder that lasted all his days. And there
is no clear evidence of any other woman
beside this Clara or Polly Woods and his
own good wife, having come at all into his
life. The impression made upon him by this
girl was quite strong enough to have lasted
on ; for Tatham has recorded how his love
for her made him ill, and how he had to be sent
for change of air to the house of the market
gardener, Boucher, at Richmond, where he
met the girl he was to marry.

The market gardener had a pretty,
" bright-eyed " daughter, named Catherine,
who, whenever her mother asked her whom
she would marry, was wont to answer,
" I have not yet seen the man." One
night she came into the room where her
family were sitting, and saw for the first
time a new comer, with young, handsome
face and flame-like hair—her own pencil
sketch is the authority—and grew upon the
moment faint, as the tale has it, from the
intuition that she saw her destined husband.
She left the room to recover, and upon her
return sat down by Blake, and heard from
his lips the story of his great love for the
false beauty, and of her fickleness and his
wretchedness. " I pity you from my heart,"
she cried. " Do you pity me ? " he an-
swered ; " then I love you for that."
Humiliated by his ill-starred love, he was
grateful for a little womanly kindness ;
and from such gratitude, not for the first time
upon the earth, sprang a love that lasted
until life had passed away. This pretty
tale has reflected itself in the great mirror
of the " Prophetic Books." In them
Pity is ever the essential thing in a woman's
soul. " The Book of Urizen " describes
thus the making of Enitharmon :

> " Wonder, awe, fear, astonishment,
> Petrify the eternal myriads
> At the first female form, now separate :
> They called her Pity, and fled."

Enitharmon is " the vegetable mortal wife

of Los ; his emanation, yet his wife till the sleep of death is passed." And the symbolic being Los, though he is Time, and more than one other great abstract thing, is also Blake himself, as may be seen by even a rapid reading of *Milton,*

When Blake had told Catherine Boucher that he loved her, he returned to his work for a year, resolved not to see her until he had put by enough to set up house upon. At the year's end, on August 13th, 1782, they were married, and began housekeeping at 23, Green Street, Leicester Fields, now Leicester Square. Mrs. Blake, knowing neither how to read nor write, had to put her mark in the register. In the course of a few years she had profited so well by her husband's teaching that she probably learnt to copy out his manuscripts ; for there is little doubt that a certain neat and formal handwriting which crops up here and there is hers, and she certainly helped to colour his illuminated books. She learnt even to see visions, beholding upon one occasion a long procession of English kings and queens pass by with silent tread. She had no children, but repaid her husband for the lack of childish voices by a love that knew no limit and a friendship that knew no flaw. In the day she would often take long walks with him, thirty miles at a stretch being no unusual distance, and having dined at a wayside inn, return under the light of the stars; and often at night, when the presences bade him get up from his bed and write, she would sit beside him, holding his hand.

A year after his marriage his first work, *Poetic Sketches*, was published at the expense of Flaxman and of some dilettanti friends, who were accustomed to gather at a Rev. Mr. Matthews', of 28, Rathbone Place. No. 28 is now a chair and umbrella mender's shop, but was then a very fashionable house on the most northernly fringe of London, upon the way to " the Jew's Harp house and the *Green Man*." The preface tells that the poems were written between the ages of twelve and twenty. He was now twenty-six, and must have been silent for these six years. He was in a period of transition. He had lost interest probably in his purely literary work, and not yet learnt to set his symbolic visions to music. The poems mark an epoch in English literature, for they were the first opening of the long-sealed well of romantic poetry; they, and not the works of Cowper and Thompson and Chatterton, being the true heralds of our modern poetry of nature and enthusiasm. There is in them no trace of mysticism, but phrases and figures of speech which were soon to pass from the metaphorical to the symbolic stage, and put on mystical significance, are very common. The singer of the " Mad Song " compares himself to a " fiend hid in a cloud ";

and we shall presently hear in definitely mystical poems of " a child upon a cloud ", and of " My brother John, the evil one, In a black cloud, making his moan " ; for cloud and vapour became to him a symbol for bodily emotions, and for the body itself. *Edward III* tells of " golden cities ", though as yet the poet knows nothing of the ages of gold, silver, and brass ; and tells of the times when the puise shall begin to beat slow,

> " And taste, and touch, and sight, and sound, and smell,
> That sing and dance round Reason's fine-wrought throne,
> Shall flee away, and leave him all forlorn "—

though as yet the poet has not learned to count and symbolize these senses, and call them " the daughters of Albion ", and draw them dancing about fallen man among the Druidic monuments of ancient Britain. (See, *Jerusalem*, page 221, and elsewhere).

A book called by its present owner, Mr. Murray, from a phrase in the first paragraph, *The Island in the Moon*, was written probably soon after the close of the six silent years. It shows in a flickering, feeble way, the dawn of the mystical period. It is a clumsy and slovenly satire upon the dilettanti and triflers who gathered about Mr. and Mrs. Matthews, but contains some lyrics not to be found elsewhere, and here reprinted from *The Works of William Blake* (B. Quaritch). The prose, touched now and then with a faint humour, has little but autobiographical interest. Of this there is, however, plenty, for the whole manuscript lightens with a blind fury against the shallow piety and shallow philosophy of his day. The thing should be read once in " The Works ", and then forgotten, for it belongs to the weak side of a strong man, to his petulance, to a certain quarrelsome self-consciousness which took hold upon him at times. There is in it a peculiar and unpleasant poem upon surgery, which was, in all likelihood, his first symbolic verse, and several poems afterwards included in " The Songs of Innocence." In 1804 he was to write of being " again enlightened by the light " which he had " enjoyed " in his youth, and which had " for exactly twenty years been closed " from him, " as by a door and window shutters." Was this darkening of the spiritual light caused by the awakening of his anger against the men and women of his time ? " The Argument " to " The Marriage of Heaven and Hell ", now soon to be written, tells how " the just man ", the imaginative man that is, walked the vale of mortal life among roses and springs of living water until the " villain ", the unimaginative man, came among the roses and the springs, and then " the just man " went forth in anger into " the wilds " among the " lions " of bitter protest. However this may be, the closing out of the light " as by a door and window shutters", if Blake's recollection do not play him false about the twenty years, the writing of "The Island of the Moon", and a quarrel with the Rathbone Place coterie, of which we have some vague record, must have come all very near together.

In 1784, upon the death of his father, William Blake moved into a house next door to the one where he had been born, and which his brother James had now inherited, and started a printseller's shop in partnership with a fellow apprentice, and took his brother Robert for apprentice to engraving. In 1787 Robert fell ill and died, Blake nursing him with such devotion that he is said to have slept for three days when the need for him was over. He had seen his brother's spirit ascending clapping its hands for joy, and might well sleep content.

Soon after the death of Robert, disagreement with his partner brought the print shop to an end, and Blake moved into neighbouring Poland Street, and started what was to prove the great work of his life. One night, a form resembling his brother Robert came to him and taught him how to engrave his poems upon copper, and how to print illustrations and decorative borderings upon the same pages with the poem. In later years he wrote to a friend, " I know that our deceased friends are more really

with us than when they are apparent to
our mortal part.   Thirteen years ago I lost a
brother, and with his spirit I converse daily
and hourly in the spirit, and see him in
remembrance in the region of my imagina-
tion.   I hear his advice, and even now write
from his dictates. Forgive me for express-
ing to you my enthusiasm, which I wish all
to partake of, since it is to me a source of
immortal joy, even in this world.   May
you continue to be so more and more, and
be more and more persuaded, that every
mortal loss is an immortal gain.   The ruins
of time build mansions in eternity."

He set to work at once to carry out the
directions of the spirit. He had now a
number of lyrics by him, and began at once
printing "The Songs of Innocence." He
drew the poems upon metal with a varnish
chiefly composed of pitch and turpentine.
The plate was then placed in a bath of acid,
and all the parts not covered by the varnish
deeply bitten, until writing and drawing stood
up in high relief, ready for ink and roller.
He then printed off the sheets in a press
for which he paid, Mr. Linnell's diary tells
us, forty pounds, and afterwards coloured,
and in some cases gilded them by hand.
All the clean legible text of song and pro-
phecy was written *backward* upon the copper
with marvellous accuracy and patience.

In 1789 appeared first "The Songs of
Innocence", and then "The Book of Thel."

illuminated missals of song in which every
page is a window open in Heaven, but 'open
not as in the days of Noah for the outpouring
of the flood " of time and space," but that
we may look into " the golden age" and
" the imagination that liveth for ever,"
and talk with those who dwell there by
" Poetry, Painting, and Music, the three
powers in man of conversing with Paradise
which the flood did not sweep away."
Alas, the poems when printed in plain black
and white, wonderful though they be, and
full of exultant peace and joyous simplicity,
give but a faint shadow of themselves as
they are in Blake's own books, where inter-
woven designs companion them, and gold
and yellow tints diffuse themselves over the
page like summer clouds. The poems
themselves are the morning song of his genius.
The thought of the world's sorrow, and that
indignation which he has called " the voice
of God ", soon began to make hoarse the
sweetness, if also to deepen the music of
his song. The third book that came from
his press, " The Marriage of Heaven and
Hell", dated 1790, has the fierce note which
never after wholly died out of his work.
It was followed in 1793 by " The Visions of
the Daughters of Albion", " America",
" Europe", " Gates of Paradise", and " The
Book of Urizen"; in 1794 by " The Songs of
Experience "; in 1795 by " The Song of Los ",
" Ahania", and in 1804 by " Jerusalem

and " Milton." He wrote also a very long
poem called " Vala " somewhere between
1797 and 1804 or 1805, but did not publish
it, probably because he shrank from the
labour and expense. It is the most splendid,
as well as the longest, of his mystical works,
and was published by Mr. E. J. Ellis and
myself, for the first time, in " The Works
of William Blake." A conception of its
luxuriant beauty can be got from the
passages quoted in this volume. There is
record too of a " Bible of Hell ", and of this
the title-page remains ; of an unfinished
poem called " The French Revolution ",
which was printed in the ordinary way, by
a certain Johnston of St. Paul's Churchyard ;
of " The Gates of Hell, for Children ", and of
an engraved book called " Othoon." The
earlier of the books which have come down
to us show the influence of Jacob Boehme
and of the kabalistic symbolism, and it is
probable that the reading of " The Morning
Redness", " Mysterium Magnum ", and stray
fragments of mediæval magical philosophy,
such as the works of Cornelius Agrippa, then
not uncommon in translation, delivered his
intellect from the spectral and formal
intellect of Swedenborg, and taught him
to think about the meaning of his own
visions. He may also have met mystics
and even students of magic, for there was
then an important secret body working in
London under three brothers named Falk.

The miniature painter Cosway, too, may have come across him, and Cosway kept a house specially for the invocation of spirits. His own illumination probably reached its height between his twentieth and his twenty-seventh year, between the close of his purely literary activity, and the shutting out of the light of the spirit " as by a door and window shutters." The six silent years may well have been silent, because the truth was coming upon him, in Boehme's beautiful phrase, " like a bursting shower." However this may be, his illumination was before all else a deliverance from Swedenborg. " The Marriage of Heaven and Hell " is certainly a reply to the latter's " Heaven and Hell ", then recently translated, and probably very audible in the talk of his Swedenborgian friend Flaxman, and of his no less Swedenborgian brother James. " A new heaven is begun," he writes on one of the first pages, " and it is now thirty-three years since its advent. The eternal hell revives, and lo, Swedenborg is the angel sitting at the tomb ; his writings are the linen clothes folded up." The creative imagination of William Blake—the Christ in him—had arisen from the tomb in the thirty-third year of his age, the year at which Christ had arisen, and with it had revived hell its activity and heaven its passivity, and the garments of theologic faith which had so long disguised it were thrown away.

The fierce invective of a later page about
Swedenborg having written no new truth,
but all the old falsehoods, combined as it is
with a glorification of the older mystics,
Boehme and Paracelsus, makes us recognize
the wrath of a man against something which
had long warped and thwarted him.   As
years went on he returned again to some
extent to the old admiration, though never
to the old subjection, until Swedenborg
became in " Milton " " strongest of men ",
" Samson shorn by the churches ", and in
" The Descriptive Catalogue " a " visionary "
whose " works " " are well worth the study of
painters and poets ", being the " foundation
of grand things."   But it must never be
forgotten that whatever Blake borrowed
from Swedenborg or Boehme, from mystic
or kabalist, he turned to his own purposes,
and transferred into a new system, growing
like a flower from its own roots, supplement-
ing in many ways, though not controverting
in any main matters, the systems of his great
predecessors, and that he stands among the
mystics of Europe beside Jacob Boehme and
the makers of the Kabala, as original as they
are and as profound.   He is one of those
great artificers of God who uttered mysteri-
ous truths to a little clan.   The others
spoke to theologians and magicians, and he
speaks to poets and artists.   The others
drew their symbols from theology and
alchemy, and he from the flowers of spring

and the leaves of summer ; but the message is the same, and the truth uttered is the truth God spake to the red clay at the beginning of the world.

The essentials of the teaching of "The Prophetic Books" can be best explained by extracts mainly from the "prose writings", for the language of the books themselves is exceedingly technical. "God is in the lowest effects as well as in the highest causes," he wrote on the margin of a copy of Lavater's "Aphorisms." "For let it be remembered that creation is God descending according to the weakness of man. Our Lord is the word of God, and everything on earth is the word of God, and in its essence is God." That portion of creation, however, which we can touch and see with our bodily senses is "infected" with the power of Satan, one of whose names is "Opacity" ; whereas that other portion which we can touch and see with the spiritual senses, and which we call "imagination", is truly, "the body of God", and the only reality ; but we must struggle to really mount towards that imaginative world, and not allow ourselves to be deceived by "memory" disguising itself as imagination. We thus mount by poetry, music, and art, which seek for ever "to cast off all that is not inspiration", and "the rotten rags of memory," and to become, "the divine members." For this reason he says that Christ's apostles were all artists, and

that " Christianity is art", and the whole
business of man is the arts," that " Israel
delivered from Egypt is art delivered from
nature and imitation " ; and that we should
all engage " before the world in some mental
pursuit." We must take some portion of
the kingdom of darkness, of the void in
which we live, and by " circumcising away
the indefinite " with a " firm and determin-
ate outline ", make of that portion a " tent
of God ", for we must always remember that
God lives alone, " in minute particulars " in
life made beautiful and graceful and vital
by imaginative significance, and that all
worthy things, all worthy deeds, all worthy
thoughts, are works of art or of imagination.
In so far as we do such works we drive the
mortality, the infection out of the things
we touch and see, and make them exist for
our spiritual senses—" the enlarged and
numerous senses "; and beholding beauty
and truth we see no more " accident and
chance ", and the indefinite void " and a
last judgment " passes over us, and the
world is consumed," for things are " burnt
up " " when you cease to behold them."

" Reason ", or argument from the memory
and from the sensations of the body, binds
us to Satan and opacity, and is the only
enemy of God. Sin awakens imagination
because it is from emotion, and is there-
fore dearer to God than reason, which is
wholly dead. Sin, however, must be

avoided, because we are prisoners, and should keep the rules of our prison house, for " you cannot have liberty in this world without what you call moral virtue, and you cannot have moral virtue without the subjection of that half of the human race who hate what you call moral virtue." But let us recognize that these laws are but " the laws of prudence ", and do not let us call them " the laws of God ", for nothing is pleasing to God except the glad invention of beautiful and exalted things. He holds it better indeed for us to break all the commandments than to sink into a dead compliance. Better any form of imaginative evil—any lust or any hate—rather than an unimaginative virtue, for " the human imagination alone " is " the divine vision and fruition " " in which man liveth eternally." " It is the human existence itself." " I care not whether a man is good or bad, " he makes Los, the " eternal mind ", say in Jerusalem ; " all that I care is whether he is a wise man or a fool. Go, put off holiness and put on intellect." By intellect he means imagination. He who recognizes imagination for his God need trouble no more about the law, for he will do naught to injure his brother, for we love all which enters truly into our imagination, and by imagination must all life become one, for a man liveth not but in his brother's face and by those " loves and tears of brothers, sisters, sons, fathers, and friends, which if man ceases to behold he ceases to exist."

The great contest of imagination with reason is described throughout " The Prophetic Books " under many symbols, but chiefly under the symbolic conflict of Los, the divine formative principle which comes midway between absolute existence and corporeal life, with Urizen, " the God of this world " and maker of dead law and blind negation. Blake considered this doctrine to be of the utmost importance, and claimed to have written it under the dictation of spiritual presences. " I have written this poem from immediate dictation," he wrote, of " Jerusalem ", " twelve or sometimes twenty or thirty lines at a time without premeditation, and even against my will. The time it has taken in writing was thus rendered non-existent, and an immense poem exists which seems the labour of a long life, all produced without labour or study." It is not possible in a short essay like the present to do more than record these things, for to discuss and to consider what these presences were would need many pages. Whatsoever they were, presences or mere imaginings, the words they dictated remain for our wonder and delight. There is not one among these words which is other than significant and precise to the laborious

student, and many passages of simple poetry
and the marvel of the pictures remain for
all who cannot or will not give the needed
labour.   Merlin's book lies open before us,
and if we cannot decipher its mysterious
symbols, then we may dream over the
melody of evocations that are not for our
conjuring, and over the strange colours
and woven forms of the spread pages.

In 1793 Blake removed to Hercules
Buildings, Lambeth, and besides the illus-
trating of "The Prophetic Books" did
there much artistic work, notably "Ne-
buchadnezzar", a huge water-colour, and
"The Lazar House", and "The Elohim
creating Adam", and a series of designs to
Young's "Night thoughts", of which a
few were printed with the poem in 1797.
The remainder are with Mr. Bain, of the
Haymarket, who very kindly shows them to
Blake's students.   The printed designs are, of
course, in plain black and white, but the rest
are faint luminous sketches in water colour.

At Lambeth, too, he saw the one ghost
of his life.   "When he was talking on
the subject of ghosts," writes Gilchrist,
"he was wont to say they did not appear
much to imaginative men, but only to
common minds who did not see the finer
spirits.   A ghost was a thing seen by the
gross bodily eye, a vision by the mental.
"Did you ever see a ghost ?" asked a
friend.   "Never but once," was the reply.

And it befell thus : Standing one evening at his garden door in Lambeth, and chancing to look up, he saw a horrible grim figure, " scaly-speckled, very awful ", stalking downstairs towards him. More frightened than ever before or after, he took to his heels and ran out of the house."

In 1800 he left London for the first time. Flaxman had introduced him to a certain Hayley, a popular poet of the day, who poured out long streams of verse, always lucid, always rational, always uninspired. He wrote prose too, and was now busy [in his turreted country house putting together a life of Cowper. Blake was invited to engrave the illustrations, and to set up house in the neighbourhood. At first all went well. The village of Felpham seemed an entirely beautiful place, beloved of God and of the spirits. Blake met all manner of kings and poets and prophets walking in shadowy multitudes on the edge of the sea, " majestic shadows, grey but luminous, and superior to the common height of man." Other and more gentle beings appeared likewise. " Did you ever see a fairy's funeral ? " said Blake to a lady who sat next him at some gathering at Hayley's or elsewhere. " Never, sir," was the answer. " I have," he replied ; " but not before last night. I was writing alone in my garden ; there was great stillness among the branches and flowers, and more than common sweetness in the air ; I heard a low and pleasant sound, and I knew not whence it came. At last I saw the broad leaf of a flower move, and underneath I saw a procession of creatures of the size and colour of green and grey grasshoppers, bearing a body laid out on a rose leaf, which they buried with songs and disappeared." He has elsewhere described the fairies as " the rulers of the vegetable world ", and " vegetable " was with him a technical term meaning " bodily " and sensuous. Jacob Boehme is also said to have had a vision of the fairies.

After a while patronage became more than he could bear, and kind worldly Hayley a burden more insistent and persistent than the grasshopper of old. Not only did Hayley himself give the prophet, who was his guest, little but mechanical work, but he sought out excellent ladies, kindly and worldly like himself, who wanted miniatures and painted fire-screens. Before long Blake began to hurl at his head petulant epigram, though there were times now and afterwards when the worldliness disappeared, and the kindliness remained alone visible to him, and then he would say that Hayley had kept him safe by his good will through spiritual terror and contests " not known to men on earth ", but which had else made the three years he spent at Felpham " the darkest years that ever mortal suffered."

Towards the last an event occurred which awoke all his slumbering gratitude. One evening he found a soldier in his garden, and not knowing that he had been put there to dig by his own gardener, asked him with all politeness to be gone. The man refused with threats, and Blake, getting angry, caught him by the elbows, and, despite his endeavour to spar, forced him away down the road to the village tavern where he was quartered. The soldier avenged himself by swearing that Blake had cursed the King, and vowed help to Bonaparte should he come over. Blake was arrested. Hayley came forward and bailed him out, and though suffering from a fall from his horse at the time, gave at the trial evidence as to character. The case was tried at the Chichester Quarter Sessions on the 11th of June, 1804, the verdict of "not guilty" awakening tumultuous applause in court. One old man remembered long afterwards Blake's flashing eyes. The soldier, whose name was Scofield, appears in "Jerusalem" as a symbol for Adam, presumably because "honest indignation", which is "the voice of God", turned him from the garden. Blake held all "natural events" to be but symbolic messages from the unknown powers. The people of Felpham remember Hayley to this day, and tradition has wrapped him about with a kind of mythological wonder, having a suggestiveness which looks like a survival from some wild tavern talk of Blake's. He had two wives, they say, and kept one in a wood with her leg chained to a tree-trunk. Blake would have made this mean the captivity of half his imagination in "the vegetable world", which is Satan's kingdom, and all nothing. The popular voice has in very truth done for Hayley what Blake himself did for Scofield. It has given him a place in mythology.

In 1804 he returned to London and took a house in South Molton Street, and there engraved "Jerusalem" and "Milton." These, with the exception of "The Ghost of Abel", a dramatic fragment written very early, but not appearing until 1822, were the last poems published by him. He continued until the end of his life to find occasional purchasers for these and other "Prophetic Books", but never any to read and understand. He did not, however, cease to write. "I have written more than Voltaire or Rousseau," he said, in one of the last years of his life; "six or seven epic poems as long as Homer, and twenty tragedies as long as *Macbeth*. . . . . I write when commanded by the spirits, and the moment I have written, I see the words fly about the room in all directions. It is then published, and the spirits can read."

Henceforth his published works were

to be wholly pictorial. He was now conscious that the " light " so long hid from him " as by a door and window shutters " was come again, and foresaw a great period of artistic creation ; for had he not conquered " the spectrous fiend " which had marred his power and obscured his inspiration ? The first works of this new and better period were done for a certain Cromeck, a publisher, who set him to illustrate Blair's " Grave." These illustrations must always remain among his greatest. They are much less illustrations of Blair than expressions of his own moods and visions. We see the body and soul rushing into each other's arms at the last day, the soul hovering over the body and exploring the recesses of the grave, and the good and bad appearing before the judgment seat of God, not as these things appeared to the orthodox eyes of Blair, but as they appeared to the mystical eyes of William Blake. The body and soul are in one aspect corporeal energy and spiritual love, and in another reason and passion, and their union is not that bodily arising from the dead, dreamed of by the orthodox, but that final peace of God wherein body and soul cry " thither " with one voice. The grave was in his eyes the sleep of reason, and the last judgment no high session of a personal law-giver, but the " casting out " of " nature " and "corporeal understanding."

Cromeck gave these designs into the hands

of Schiavonetti, an excellent engraver, but a follower of the fashionable school of "blots and blurs", of soft shadows and broken lights, and not of the unfashionable school of "firm and determinate outline" to which Blake belonged. Blake likewise had been promised the engraving, and the choice of another was a serious money loss to him. The result was a quarrel, which grew to the utmost vehemence when Cromeck added the further wrong of setting Stothard to paint for engraving a picture of "The Canterbury Pilgrims", having taken the idea from seeing Blake at work on the same subject with like intentions. Blake tried to vindicate himself by an exhibition of his paintings, "The Canterbury Pilgrims" among them. The exhibition was held at his brother James', in Golden Square, in 1809, and proved an utter failure. I give many extracts from the printed catalogue and from an address to the public, which never got beyond the MS. stage. Both catalogue and address are full of magnificent and subtle irony and of violent and petulant anger. He would not moderate his passion, for he was ever combative against a time which loved moderation, compromise, and measured phrase, because it was a time of "unbelief and fear" and of imaginative dearth. Had he not said, "bring out number, weight, and measure in a time of dearth"? and with him there was no dearth ; and also that "the road of excess leads to the palace of wisdom" ? His fault was not that he did net moderate his passion, but that he did not feel the error he so often warns himself against, of being angry with individuals instead of "states" of mind. The evil he denounced was really evil, but the men he denounced did not really personify that evil. The turbulent heart of the mystic could not but feel wrath against a time that knew not him or his. No wonder that he should fall, from sheer despair of making any man understand his subtle philosophy of life, into many an unsubtle unphilosophical rhapsody of hate when too angry even to hide himself in storm clouds of paradox. He had probably never seen any good painting of the Florentine and Flemish schools, but holding them to be the source of the art of his day, denounced them with violence. Had they not sacrificed the intellectual outline to indefinite lights and shadows, and renounced imaginative things for what seemed to him unimaginative copying of corporeal life and lifeless matter ? Were they not his enemies in all things, and the enemies of Raphael and Angelo and Durer ? He made, in a blind hopeless way, something of the same protest made afterwards by the pre-Raphaelites with more success. They saw nothing but an artistic issue, and were at peace ; whereas he saw

in every issue the whole contest of light
and darkness, and found no peace. To
him the universe seemed filled with an in-
tense excitement at once infinitesimal and
infinite, for in every grass blade, in every
atom of dust, Los, the "eternal mind",
warred upon dragon Urizen, "the God of
this world." The "dots and lozenges",
and the "indefinite" shadows of engraver
or painter, took upon them portentous
meanings to his visionary eyes. "I know
that the great majority of Englishmen are
fond of the indefinite," he writes to a
correspondent, "which they measure by
Newton's doctrine of the fluxions of an
atom, a thing which does not exist" (that
is to say, belongs to reason, not to imagina-
tion; to nature, not to mind). "These
are politicians, and think that Republican
art" (a system of thought or art which
gives every one of the parts separate in-
dividuality and separate rights as in a
Republic) "is inimical to their atom, for a
line or lineament is not formed by chance.
A line is a line in its minutest subdivisions,
straight or crooked. It is itself, not inter-
measurable by anything else. . . . . But
since the French Revolution Englishmen
are all intermeasurable by one another,
certainly a happy state of agreement in
which I for one do not agree." "The
dots or lozenges", "the blots and blurs",
have no individuality when taken apart, and

what is true of them is true also of the men
for whom " the blots and blurs " are made ;
for are not all things symbolic, and is not
art the greatest of symbols ?   In his philo-
sophy, as expounded in " The Prophetic
Books ", he had a place for everything,
even for " nature " and the corporeal hind-
rance, but he left a place for the highest
only in his interpretation of the philosophy,
and forgot that we must never be partisans,
not even partisans of the spirit.

For a time now his purse was very empty,
he and his wife, if Cromeck is to be believed,
which he probably is not, living for a time
on 10s. a week, and it might, perhaps, have
kept empty to the end had not he met in
1818 John Linnell, the landscape painter,
and found in him the most generous patron
of his life.   Now, too, he made the acquaint-
ance of another good friend, John Varley,
" the father of modern water-colour ",
and did for him a series of drawings of his
spiritual visitants : " The Ghost of a Flea "
(a symbol of the rapacious man), " The Man
who built the Pryamids " (a symbol prob-
ably of the man of worldly power, for Egypt
is nature or the world, and the pyramids a
glory of Egypt), and many others.   In 1821
he moved from Poland Street to Fountain
Court, and made for Mr. Linnell the famous
series of designs, to " Job ", which is perhaps
his masterpiece.   Their austere majesty,
too well known to need any description

here, contrasts with the fanciful prettiness
and delicate grace of his early work. Life
had touched his imagination with melan-
choly. He received £100 for the plates,
and was to get another £100 out of the
profits of publication. He got £50 of this
second £100 before his death, the slow sale
not making a bigger sum possible. In
1822 he painted a very fine series of water-
colours illustrating "Paradise Lost" for
Mr. Linnell, filling them with the peculiari-
ties of his own illumination as usual, and
in 1825 began an immense series of designs
to "Dante" for the same friend, sketching
them in water-colour and engraving seven.
Of those he engraved, "Francesco and
Paola" is the most perfect and the most
moving, and must always haunt the memory
with a beauty at once tender and august.
Had he lived to finish the whole series, or
even the hundred and odd drawings he
began, it had surely been the veritable
crown of his labours as an artist; but he
was to pass the gate he had called "of pearl
and gold", and to stand where Dante stood
by Beatrice, and to enter the great white
Rose before his hands had half transcribed
the story of that other mystic traveller.
In 1827 he fell ill of a strange complaint, a
shivering and sinking, which told him he
had not long to live. He wrote to a friend,
"I have been very near the gates of death,
and have returned very weak, and an old

man, feeble and tottering, but not in spirit
and life, not in the real man, the imagina-
tion which liveth for ever. In that I grow
stronger and stronger as this foolish body
decays " ; and then passed on to discuss
matters of business, and matters of engrav-
ing and politics, but soon burst out again.
" Flaxman is gone, and we must soon
follow every one to his own eternal house,
leaving the delusions of Goddess Nature
and her laws to get into freedom from
all the laws of the numbers—into the mind
in which every one is king and priest in his
own house. God grant it on earth as it is
in heaven."

" On the day of his death," writes a friend
who had his account from Mrs. Blake,
" he composed songs to his Maker, so
sweetly to the ear of his Catherine, that,
when she stood to hear him, he, looking
upon her most affectionately, said, " My
beloved ! they are *not mine*. *No !* They
are *not* mine." He told her they would not
be parted ; he should always be about her
to take care of her." Another account
says, " he said he was going to that country
he had all his life wished to see, and expressed
himself happy, hoping for salvation through
Jesus Christ. Just before he died his
countenance became fair, his eyes brightened
and he burst out into singing of the things
he saw in heaven." " He made the rafters
ring," said Tatham. " The death of a

saint," said a poor woman who had come in to help Mrs. Blake.

The wife continued to believe him always with her in the spirit, even calling out to him at times as if he were but a few yards away ; but, none the less, fretted herself into the grave, surviving him only two years. No spiritual companionship could make up for the lack of daily communion in the common things of life, for are we not one half " phantoms of the earth and water ? " She left his designs and unpublished manuscripts, of which there were, according to Allan Cunningham, a hundred volumes ready for the press, to Tatham, who had shown her no little friendliness. Tatham was an " angel " in the Irvingite Church, and coming to hold that the designs and poems alike were inspired by the devil, pronounced sentence upon them, and gave up two days to their burning. " I have," wrote Blake, " always found that angels have the vanity to speak of themselves as the only wise ; this they do with a confident insolence sprouting from systematic reasoning." Though Tatham, bound in by systematic theology, did him well nigh the greatest wrong one man can do another, none the less is Tatham's MS. life of Blake a long cry of admiration. He speaks of " his noble and elastic mind ", of his profound and beautiful talk, and of his varied knowledge. Yet, alas, could he only have convinced himself that it was not for him to judge whether, when Blake wrote of vision "a bad cause" —to use his own phrase, "made a bad book "—we might still have that account of Genesis, "as understood by a Christian visionary", of which a passage, when read out, seemed "striking", even to conventional Crab Robinson, and perhaps "The Book of Moonlight", a work upon art, though for this I do not greatly long, and the "Othoon", and many lyrics and designs, whereof the very names are dead. Blake himself would have felt little anger, for he had thought of burning his MS. himself, holding, perhaps as Boehme held, and Swedenborg also, that there were many great things best unuttered within earshot of the world. Boehme held himself permitted to speak of much only among his "schoolfellows"; and Blake held there were listeners in other worlds than this. He knew, despite the neglect and scorn of his time, that fame even upon the earth would be granted him, and that his work was done, for the Eternal Powers do not labour in vain.

> " Re-engraved time after time,
> Ever in their youthful prime ;
> My designs unchanged remain,
> Time may rage but rage in vain.
> For above Time's troubled fountains,
> On the great Atlantic mountains,
> In my golden house on high,
> There they shine eternally."

W. B. YEATS.

I HAVE to thank Mr. E. J. Ellis for lending me his copy of " the MS. book," and for kindly reading the proofs of my introduction : Mr. Fairfax Murray for leave to reprint three lyrics from "The Island of the Moon" ; and Dr. Carter Blake for information about Blake's ancestry.

FROM THE POETICAL SKETCHES.

POETICAL SKETCHES.

TO SPRING.

O THOU with dewy locks, who lookest down
Through the clear windows of the morning, turn
Thine angel eyes upon our western isle,
Which in full choir hails thy approach, O Spring !

The hills tell each other, and the listening
Valleys hear ; all our longing eyes are turned
Up to thy bright pavilions : issue forth,
And let thy holy feet visit our clime !

Come o'er the eastern hills, and let our winds
Kiss thy perfumèd garments ; let us taste
Thy morn and evening breath ; scatter thy pearls
Upon our lovesick land that mourns for thee.

O deck her forth with thy fair fingers ; pour
Thy soft kisses on her bosom ; and put
Thy golden crown upon her languished head,
Whose modest tresses were bound up for thee !

TO SUMMER.

O THOU who passest through our valleys in
Thy strength, curb thy fierce steeds, allay the heat
That flames from their large nostrils ! Thou, O
    Summer,

Oft pitched'st here thy golden tent, and oft
Beneath our oaks hast slept, while we beheld
With joy thy ruddy limbs and flourishing hair.

Beneath our thickest shades we oft have heard
Thy voice, when Noon upon his fervid car
Rode o'er the deep of heaven.   Beside our springs
Sit down, and in our mossy valleys, on
Some bank beside a river clear, throw thy
Silk draperies off, and rush into the stream !
Our valleys love the Summer in his pride.

Our bards are famed who strike the silver wire ;
Our youth are bolder than the southern swains,
Our maidens fairer in the sprightly dance.
We lack not songs, nor instruments of joy,
Nor echoes sweet, nor waters clear as heaven,
Nor laurel wreaths against the sultry heat.

TO AUTUMN.

O Autumn, laden with fruit, and stained
With the blood of the grape, pass not, but sit
Beneath my shady roof ; there thou may'st rest,
And tune thy jolly voice to my fresh pipe.
And all the daughters of the year shall dance !
Sing now the lusty song of fruits and flowers.

" The narrow bud opens her beauties to
The sun, and love runs in her thrilling veins ;
Blossoms hang round the brows of Morning, and
Flourish down the bright cheek of modest Eve,
Till clust'ring Summer breaks forth into singing,
And feathered clouds strew flowers round her head.

" The Spirits of the Air live on the smells
Of fruit ; and Joy, with pinions light, roves round
The gardens, or sits singing in the trees,"
Thus sang the jolly Autumn as he sat ;
Then rose, girded himself, and o'er the bleak
Hills fled from our sight : but left his golden load.

TO WINTER.

O WINTER ! bar thine adamantine doors :
The North is thine ; there hast thou built thy dark
Deep-founded habitation.   Shake not thy roofs,
Nor bend thy pillars with thine iron car.

He hears me not, but o'er the yawning deep
Rides heavy ; his storms are unchainèd, sheathed
In ribbèd steel ; I dare not lift mine eyes ;
For he hath reared his sceptre o'er the world.

Lo ! now the direful monster, whose skin clings
To his strong bones, strides o'er the groaning rocks :
He withers all in silence, and in his hand
Unclothes the earth, and freezes up frail life.

He takes his seat upon the cliffs,—the mariner
Cries in vain.   Poor little wretch, that deal'st
With storms !—till heaven smiles, and the monster
Is driv'n yelling to his caves beneath Mount Hecla.

TO THE EVENING STAR.

THOU fair-haired Angel of the Evening,
Now, whilst the sun rests on the mountains, light
Thy bright torch of love : thy radiant crown
Put on, and smile upon our evening bed !

Smile on our loves : and, while thou drawest the
Blue curtains of the sky, scatter thy silver dew
On every flower that shuts its sweet eyes
In timely sleep.   Let thy west wind sleep on
The lake : speak silence with thy glimmering eyes,
And wash the dusk with silver.—Soon, full soon,
Dost thou withdraw ; then the wolf rages wide,
And then the lion glares through the dun forest.
The fleeces of our flocks are covered with
Thy sacred dew : protect them with thine influence !

TO MORNING.

O HOLY virgin, clad in purest white,
Unlock heaven's golden gates, and issue forth ;
Awake the dawn that sleeps in heaven ; let light
Rise from the chambers of the East, and bring
The honeyed dew that cometh on waking day.
O radiant Morning, salute the Sun,
Roused like a huntsman to the chase, and with
Thy buskined feet appear upon our hills.

SONG.

How sweet I roamed from field to field,
    And tasted all the summer's pride,
Till I the Prince of Love beheld
    Who in the sunny beams did glide.

He showed me lilies for my hair,
    And blushing roses for my brow ;
He led me through his gardens fair
    Where all his golden pleasure grow.

With sweet May-dews my wings were wet,
   And Phœbus fired my vocal rage ;
He caught me in his silken net,
   And shut me in his golden cage.

He loves to sit and hear me sing,
   Then, laughing, sports and plays with me,
Then stretches out my golden wing,
   And mocks my loss of liberty.

SONG.

My silks and fine array,
   My smiles and languished air,
By love are driven away ;
   And mournful lean Despair
Brings me yew to deck my grave ;
Such end true lovers have.

His face is fair as heaven
   When springing buds unfold ;
O why to him was't given,
   Whose heart is wintry cold ?
His breast is love's all-worshipped tomb,
Where all love's pilgrims come.

Bring me an axe and spade,
   Bring me a winding-sheet ;
When I my grave have made,
   Let winds and tempests beat :
Then down I'll lie, as cold as clay.
True love doth pass away !

SONG.

Love and harmony combine,
And around our souls entwine,
While thy branches mix with mine,
And our roots together join.

Joys upon our branches sit,
Chirping loud and singing sweet;
Like gentle streams beneath our feet,
Innocence and virtue meet.

Thou the golden fruit dost bear,
I am clad in flowers fair;
Thy sweet boughs perfume the air,
And the turtle buildeth there.

There she sits and feeds her young
Sweet I hear her mournful song;
And thy lovely leaves among
There is Love; I hear his tongue.

There his charming nest doth lay,
There he sleeps the night away;
There he sports along the day,
And doth among our branches play.

SONG.

I love the jocund dance,
  The softly-breathing song,
Where innocent eyes do glance,
  And where lisps the maiden's tongue.

I love the laughing vale,
  I love the echoing hill,
Where mirth does never fail,
  And the jolly swain laughs his fill.

I love the pleasant cot,
  I love the innocent bower,
Where white and brown is our lot,
  Or fruit in the mid-day hour.

I love the oaken seat
  Beneath the oaken tree,
Where all the old villagers meet,
  And laugh our sports to see.

I love our neighbours all,—
  But, Kitty, I better love thee :
And love them I ever shall,
  But thou art all to me.

SONG.

MEMORY, hither come,
  And tune your merry notes :
And, while upon the wind
  Your music floats,
I'll pore upon the stream
Where sighing lovers dream,
And fish for fancies as they pass
Within the watery glass.

I'll drink of the clear stream,
  And hear the linnet's song,
And there I'll lie and dream
  The day along :

And, when night comes, I'll go
To places fit for woe,
Walking along the darkened valley
With silent Melancholy.

MAD SONG.

The wild winds weep,
   And the night is a-cold ;
Come hither, Sleep,
   And my griefs enfold !. . . .
But lo ! the morning peeps
Over the eastern steeps,
And the rustling birds of dawn
The earth do scorn.

Lo ! to the vault
   Of pavèd heaven,
With sorrow fraught,
   My notes are driven ;
They strike the ear of Night,
Make weep the eyes of Day ;
They make mad the roaring winds,
   And with tempests play.

Like a fiend in a cloud,
   With howling woe
After night I do crowd
   And with night will go ;
I turn my back to the east
From whence comforts have increased ;
For light doth seize my brain
With frantic pain.

SONG.

FRESH from the dewy hill, the merry Year
Smiles on my head, and mounts his flaming car :
Round my young brows the laurel wreathes a shade,
And rising glories beam around my head.

My feet are winged, while o'er the dewy lawn
I meet my maiden risen like the morn.
O bless those holy feet, like angel's feet ;
O bless those limbs, beaming with heavenly light !

Like as an angel glittering in the sky
In times of innocence and holy joy ;
The joyful shepherd stops his grateful song
To hear the music of an angel's tongue.

So, when she speaks, the voice of Heaven I hear ;
So, when we walk, nothing impure comes near ;
Each field seems Eden, and each calm retreat ;
Each village seems the haunt of holy feet.

But, that sweet village where my black-eyed maid
Closes her eyes in sleep beneath night's shade
Whene'er I enter, more than mortal fire
Burns in my soul, and does my song inspire.

SONG.

WHEN early morn walks forth in sober grey,
Then to my black-eyed maid I haste away.
When Evening sits beneath her dusky bower,
And gently sighs away the silent hour,
The village bell alarms, away I go,
And the vale darkens at my pensive woe.

To that sweet village where my black-eyed maid
Doth drop a tear beneath the silent shade
I turn my eyes ; and pensive as I go
Curse my black stars, and bless my pleasing woe.

Oft, when the Summer sleeps among the trees,
Whispering faint murmurs to the scanty breeze,
I walk the village round ; if at her side
A youth doth walk in stolen joy and pride,
I curse my stars in bitter grief and woe,
That made my love so high, and me so low.

O should she e'er prove false, his limbs I'd tear
And throw all pity on the burning air !
I'd curse bright fortune for my mixèd lot,
And then I'd die in peace, and be forgot.

TO THE MUSES.

WHETHER on Ida's shady brow,
    Or in the chambers of the East,
The chambers of the Sun, that now
    From ancient melody have ceased ;

Whether in heaven ye wander fair,
    Or the green corners of the earth,
Or the blue regions of the air
    Where the melodious winds have birth ;

Whether on crystal rocks ye rove,
    Beneath the bosom of the sea,
Wandering in many a coral grove ;
    Fair Nine, forsaking Poetry ;

How have you left the ancient love
　　That bards of old enjoyed in you !
The languid strings do scarcely move,
　　The sound is forced, the notes are few !

AN IMITATION OF SPENSER.

GOLDEN Apollo, that through heaven wide
　　Scatter'st the rays of light, and truth his beams,
In lucent words my darkling verses dight,
　　And wash my earthy mind in thy clear streams,
　　That wisdom may descend in fairy dreams,
All while the jocund Hours in thy train
　　Scatter their fancies at thy poet's feet :
And, when thou yield'st to Night thy wide domain,
Let rays of truth enlight his sleeping brain.

For brutish Pan in vain might thee assay
　　With tinkling sounds to dash thy nervous verse,
Sound without sense ; yet in his rude affray
　　(For Ignorance is Folly's leasing nurse,
　　And love of Folly needs none other's curse)
Midas the praise hath gained of lengthened ears,
　　For which himself might deem him ne'er the worse
To sit in council with his modern peers,
　　And judge of tinkling rhymes and elegances terse.

And thou, Mercurius, that with wingèd bow
　　Dost mount aloft into the yielding sky,
And through heaven's halls thy airy flight dost throw,
　　Entering with holy feet to where on high

Jove weighs the counsel of futurity ;
Then, laden with eternal fate, dost go
    Down, like a falling star, from autumn sky,
    And o'er the surface of the silent deep dost fly :

If thou arrivest at the sandy shore
    Where nought but envious hissing adders dwell,
Thy golden rod, thrown on the dusty floor,
    Can charm to harmony with potent spell ;
    Such is sweet eloquence, that does dispel
Envy and Hate, that thirst for human gore ;
    And cause in sweet society to dwell
    Vile savage minds that lurk in lonely cell.

O Mercury, assist my labouring sense
    That round the circle of the world would fly,
As the wing'd eagle scorns the towery fence
    Of Alpine hills round his high aëry,
    And searches through the corners of the sky,
Sports in the clouds to hear the thunder's sound,
    And see the wingèd lightnings as they fly ;
Then, bosomed in an amber cloud, around
    Plumes his wide wings, and seeks Sol's palace high.

And thou, O warrior-maid invincible,
    Armed with the terrors of almighty Jove,
Pallas, Minerva, maiden terrible,
    Lov'st thou to walk the peaceful solemn grove,
    In solemn gloom of branches interwove ?
Or bear'st thy ægis o'er the burning field,
    Where like the sea the waves of battle move ?
Or have thy soft piteous eyes beheld
    The weary wanderer through the desert rove ?
    Or does the afflicted man thy heavenly bosom move ?

BLIND-MAN'S BUFF.

WHEN silver snow decks Susan's clothes,
And jewel hangs at th' shepherd's nose,
The blushing bank is all my care,
With hearth so red, and walls so fair.
" Heap the sea-coal, come, heap it higher ;
The oaken log lay on the fire."
The well-washed stools, a circling row,
With lad and lass, how fair the show !
The merry can of nut-brown ale,
The laughing jest, the love-sick tale,—
Till, tired of chat, the game begins.
The lasses prick the lads with pins.
Roger from Dolly twitched the stool ;
She, falling, kissed the ground, poor fool !
She blushed so red, with sidelong glance
At hobnail Dick, who grieved the chance.
But now for Blind-man's Buff they call ;
Of each incumbrance clear the hall.

Jenny her silken 'kerchief folds,
And blear-eyed Will the black lot holds.
Now laughing stops, with " Silence, hush ! "
And Peggy Pout gives Sam a push.
The Blind-man's arms, extended wide,
Sam slips between :—" Oh woe betide
Thee, clumsy Will ! "—But tittering Kate
Is penned up in the corner strait !
And now Will's eyes beheld the play ;
He thought his face was t'other way.
" Now, Kitty, now ! what chance has thou ?
Roger so near thee trips, I vow ! "

She catches him—then Roger ties
His own head up—but not his eyes ;
For through the slender cloth he sees,
And runs at Sam, who slips with ease
His clumsy hold ; and, dodging round,
Sukey is tumbled on the ground.—
" See what it is to play unfair !
Where cheating is, there's mischief there."
But Roger still pursues the chase,—
" He sees ! he sees ! " cries softly Grace ;
" O Roger, thou, unskilled in art,
Must, surer bound, go through thy part ! "

Now Kitty, pert, repeats the rhymes,
And Roger turns him round three times.
Then pauses ere he starts.   But Dick
Was mischief-bent upon a trick :
Down on his hands and knees he lay
Directly in the Blind-man's way,
Then cries out " Hem ! "—Hodge heard, and ran
With hoodwinked chance—sure of his man ;
But down he came.—Alas, how frail
Our best of hopes, how soon they fail !
With crimson drops he stains the ground :
Confusion startles all around.
Poor piteous Dick supports his head,
And fain would cure the hurt he made.
But Kitty hasted with a key,
And down his back they straight convey
The cold relief ; the blood is stayed,
And Hodge again holds up his head.

Such are the fortunes of the game ;
And those who play should stop the same

By wholesome laws, such as—All those
Who on the blinded man impose
Stand in his stead ; as, long agone
When men were first a nation grown,
Lawless they lived, till wantonness
And liberty began to increase,
And one man lay in another's way ;
Then laws were made to keep fair play.

KING EDWARD THE THIRD.

PERSONS.

KING EDWARD.	SIR THOMAS DAGWORTH.
THE BLACK PRINCE.	SIR WALTER MANNY.
QUEEN PHILIPPA.	LORD AUDLEY.
DUKE OF CLARENCE.	LORD PERCY.
SIR JOHN CHANDOS.	BISHOP.

WILLIAM, *Dagworth's man.*
PETER BLUNT, *a common soldier.*

SCENE, *The Coast of France.*

KING EDWARD *and Nobles before it.   The Army.*

KING.

O THOU to whose fury the nations are
But as dust ! maintain thy servant's right.
Without thine aid, the twisted mail, and spear,
And forgèd helm, and shield of seven times beaten
    brass,
Are idle trophies of the vanquisher.
When confusion rages, when the field is in a flame,
When the cries of blood tear horror from heaven,
And yelling Death runs up and down the ranks,

Let Liberty, the chartered right of Englishmen,
Won by our fathers in many a glorious field,
Enerve my soldiers ; let Liberty
Blaze in each countenance, and fire the battle.
The enemy fight in chains, invisible chains, but heavy ;
Their minds are fettered ; then how can they be free ?
While, like the mounting flame,
We spring to battle o'er the floods of death !
And these fair youths, the flower of England,
Vent'ring their lives in my most righteous cause,
Oh sheathe their hearts with triple steel, that they
May emulate their fathers' virtues !
And thou, my son, be strong ; thou fightest for a
     crown
That death can never ravish from thy brow,
A crown of glory ; but from thy very dust
Shall beam a radiance, to fire the breasts
Of youth unborn ! Our names are written equal
In Fame's wide-trophied hall ; 'tis ours to gild
The letters, and to make them shine with gold
That never tarnishes : whether Third Edward,
Or the Prince of Wales, or Montacute, or Mortimer,
Or ev'n the least by birth, shall gain the brightest
     fame,
Is in His hand to whom all men are equal.
The world of men are like the numerous stars
That beam and twinkle in the depth of night,
Each clad in glory according to his sphere ;
But we, that wander from our native seats
And beam forth lustre on a darkling world,
Grow larger as we advance : and some perhaps,
The most obscure at home, that scarce were seen
To twinkle in their sphere, may so advance

That the astonished world, with upturned eyes,
Regardless of the moon, and those that once were
    bright,
Stand only for to gaze upon their splendour.
    [*He here knights the Prince and other young Nobles.*
Now let us take a just revenge for those
Brave lords who fell beneath the bloody axe
At Paris.   Thanks, noble Harcourt, for 'twas
By your advice we landed here in Brittany,
A country not yet sown with destruction,
And where the fiery whirlwind of swift war
Has not yet swept its desolating wing.—
Into three parties we divide by day,
And separate march, but join again at night :
Each knows his rank, and Heaven marshal all.
                      [*Exeunt.*

      SCENE, *English Court.*

LIONEL, DUKE OF CLARENCE, QUEEN PHILIPPA,
      Lords, Bishop, Etc.

      CLARENCE.

My Lords, I have by the advice of her
Whom I am doubly bound to obey, my parent
And my sovereign, called you together.
My task is great, my burden heavier than
My unfledged years ;
Yet with your kind assistance, Lords, I hope
England shall dwell in peace : that, while my father
Toils in his wars, and turns his eyes on this
His native shore, and sees Commerce fly round
With his white wings, and sees his golden London
And her silver Thames, thronged with shining spires

And corded ships, her merchants buzzing round
Like summer bees, and all the golden cities
In his land overflowing with honey,
Glory may not be dimmed with clouds of care.
Say, Lords, should not our thoughts be first to com-
    merce ?
My Lord Bishop, you would recommend us agricul-
    ture ?

BISHOP.

Sweet Prince, the arts of peace are great,
And no less glorious than those of war,
Perhaps more glorious, in the philosophic mind.
When I sit at my home, a private man,
My thoughts are on my gardens and my fields,
How to employ the hand that lacketh bread.
If Industry is in my diocese,
Religion will flourish ; each man's heart
Is cultivated and will bring forth fruit :
This is my private duty and my pleasure.
But, as I sit in council with my prince,
My thoughts take in the general good of the whole,
And England is the land favoured by Commerce ;
For Commerce, though the child of Agriculture,
Fosters his parent, who else must sweat and toil,
And gain but scanty fare. Then, my dear Lord,
Be England's trade our care ; and we, as tradesmen
Looking to the gain of this our native land.

CLARENCE.

O my good Lord, true wisdom drops like honey
From your tongue, as from a worshipped oak !
Forgive, my Lords, my talkative youth, that speaks

Not merely what my narrow observation has
Pick'd up, but what I have concluded from your
    lessons.
Now, by the Queen's advice, I ask your leave
To dine to-morrow with the Mayor of London ;
If I obtain your leave, I have another boon
To ask, which is, the favour of your company.
I fear Lord Percy will not give me leave.

PERCY.

Dear Sir, a prince should always keep his state,
And grant his favours with a sparing hand,
Or they are never rightly valuèd.
These are my thoughts : yet it were best to go :
But keep a proper dignity, for now
You represent the sacred person of
Your father ; 'tis with princes as 'tis with the sun ;
If not sometimes o'erclouded, we grow weary
Of his officious glory.

CLARENCE.

Then you will give me leave to shine sometimes,
My Lord ?

LORD (*aside*).

Thou hast a gallant spirit, which I fear
Will be imposed on by the closer sort.

CLARENCE.

Well, I'll endeavour to take
Lord Percy's advice ; I have been used so much
To dignity that I'm sick on't.

QUEEN PHILIPPA.

Fie, fie, Lord Clarence! you proceed not to business,
But speak of your own pleasures.
I hope their lordships will excuse your giddiness.

CLARENCE.

My Lords, the French have fitted out many
Small ships of war that, like to ravening wolves,
Infest our English seas, devouring all
Our burdened vessels, spoiling our naval flocks.
The merchants do complain, and beg our aid.

PERCY.

The merchants are rich enough ;
Can they not help themselves ?

BISHOP.

They can, and may ; but how to gain their will
Requires our countenance and help.

PERCY.

When that they find they must, my Lord, they will :
Let them but suffer awhile, and you shall see
They will bestir themselves.

BISHOP.

Lord Percy cannot mean that we should suffer
This disgrace.   If so, we are not sovereigns
Of the sea ; our right that Heaven gave
To England, when at the birth of Nature
She was seated in the deep ; the Ocean ceased
His mighty roar, and, fawning, played around
Her snowy feet, and owned his awful Queen.

Lord Percy, if the heart is sick, the head
Must be aggrieved ; if but one member suffer,
The heart doth fail. You say, my Lord, the mer-
　　chants
Can, if they will, defend themselves against
These rovers : this is a noble scheme,
Worthy the brave Lord Percy, and as worthy
His generous aid to put it into practice.

PERCY.

Lord Bishop, what was rash in me is wise
In you ; I dare not own the plan. 'Tis not
Mine. Yet will I, if you please,
Quickly to the Lord Mayor, and work him onward
To this most glorious voyage ; on which cast
I'll set my whole estate,
But we will bring these Gallic rovers under.

QUEEN PHILIPPA.

Thanks, brave Lord Percy ; you have the thanks
Of England's Queen, and will, ere long, of England.
　　　　　　　　　　　　　　　　　　[Exeunt.

SCENE, *At Cressy.*

SIR THOMAS DAGWORTH *and* LORD AUDLEY *meeting.*

AUDLEY.

Good-morrow, brave Sir Thomas ; the bright morn
Smiles on our army, and the gallant sun
Springs from the hills like a young hero

Into the battle, shaking his golden locks
Exultingly : this is a promising day.

DAGWORTH.

Why, my Lord Audley, I don't know.
Give me your hand, and now I'll tell you what
I think you do not know.   Edward's afraid of Philip.

AUDLEY.

Ha, ha ! Sir Thomas ! you but joke ;
Did you e'er see him fear ? At Blanchetaque,
When almost singly he drove six thousand
French from the ford, did he fear then ?

DAGWORTH.

Yes, fear.   That made him fight so.

AUDLEY.

By the same reason I might say 'tis fear
That makes you fight.

DAGWORTH.

Mayhap you may.   Look upon Edward's face,
No one can say he fears ; but, when he turns
His back, then I will say it to his face ;
He is afraid : he makes us all afraid.
I cannot bear the enemy at my back.
Now here we are at Cressy ; where to-morrow,
To-morrow we shall know.   I say, Lord Audley,
That Edward runs away from Philip.

AUDLEY.

Perhaps you think the Prince too is afraid ?

DAGWORTH.

No ; God forbid ! I am sure he is not.
He is a young lion. Oh I have seen him fight
And give command, and lightning has flashed
From his eyes across the field : I have seen him
Shake hands with Death, and strike a bargain for
The enemy ; he has danced in the field
Of battle, like the youth at morris-play.
I'm sure he's not afraid, nor Warwick, nor none,
None of us but me, and I am very much afraid.

AUDLEY.

Are you afraid, too, Sir Thomas ?
I believe that as much as I believe
The King's afraid ; but what are you afraid of ?

DAGWORTH.

Of having my back laid open ; we turn
Our backs to the fire, till we shall burn our skirts.

AUDLEY.

And this, Sir Thomas, you call fear ? Your fear
Is of a different kind, then, from the King's ;
He fears to turn his face, and you to turn your back.
I do not think, Sir Thomas, you know what fear is.

Enter Sir John Chandos.

CHANDOS.

Good-morrow, Generals ; I give you joy :
Welcome to the fields of Cressy. Here we stop,
And wait for Philip.

DAGWORTH.

I hope so.

AUDLEY.

There, Sir Thomas ; do you call that fear ?

DAGWORTH.

I don't know ; perhaps he takes it by fits.
Why, noble Chandos, look you here—
One rotten sheep spoils the whole flock ;
And if the bell-wether is tainted, I wish
The Prince may not catch the distemper too.

CHANDOS.

Distemper, Sir Thomas ! What distemper ?
I have not heard.

DAGWORTH.

Why, Chandos, you are a wise man,
I know you understand me ; a distemper
The King caught here in France of running away.

AUDLEY.

Sir Thomas, you say you have caught it too.

DAGWORTH.

And so will the whole army ; 'tis very catching,
For, when the coward runs, the brave man totters
Perhaps the air of the country is the cause.
I feel it coming upon me, so I strive against it ;
You yet are whole ; but, after a few more
Retreats, we all shall know how to retreat
Better than fight.—To be plain, I think retreating
Too often takes away a soldier's courage.

CHANDOS.

Here comes the King himself : tell him your thoughts
Plainly, Sir Thomas.

DAGWORTH.

I've told him before, but his disorder
Has made him deaf.

    Enter KING EDWARD *and* BLACK PRINCE.

KING.

Good-morrow, Generals ; when English courage fails
Down goes our right to France.
But we are conquerors everywhere ; nothing
Can stand our soldiers ; each man is worthy
Of a triumph. Such an army of heroes
Ne'er shouted to the heavens, nor shook the field.
Edward, my son, thou art
Most happy, having such command : the man
Were base who were not fired to deeds
Above heroic, having such examples.

PRINCE.

Sire, with respect and deference I look
Upon such noble souls, and wish myself
Worthy the high command that Heaven and you
Have given me. When I have seen the field glow.
And in each countenance the soul of war
Curbed by the manliest reason, I have been winged
With certain victory ; and 'tis my boast,
And shall be still my glory, I was inspired
By these brave troops.

DAGWORTH.

      Your Grace had better make
Them all Generals.

KING.

Sir Thomas Dagworth, you must have your joke,
And shall, while you can fight as you did at
The Ford.

DAGWORTH.

I have a small petition to your Majesty.

KING.

What can Sir Thomas Dagworth ask that Edward
Can refuse ?

DAGWORTH.

I hope your Majesty cannot refuse so great
A trifle ; I've gilt your cause with my best blood,
And would again, were I not forbid
By him whom I am bound to obey : my hands
Are tied up, my courage shrunk and withered,
My sinews slackened, and my voice scarce heard ;
Therefore I beg I may return to England.

KING.

I know not what you could have asked, Sir Thomas,
That I would not have sooner parted with
Than such a soldier as you have been, and such a
    friend :
Nay, I will know the most remote particulars
Of this your strange petition ; that, if I can,
I still may keep you here.

DAGWORTH.

Here on the fields of Cressy we are settled
Till Philip springs the timorous covey again.
The wolf is hunted down by causeless fear ;

The lion flees, and fear usurps his heart,
Startled, astonished at the clamorous cock ;
The eagle, that doth gaze upon the sun,
Fears the small fire that plays about the fen.
If, at this moment of their idle fear,
The dog doth seize the wolf, the forester the lion,
The negro in the crevice of the rock
Doth seize the soaring eagle ; undone by flight,
They tame submit ; such the effect flight has
On noble souls.   Now hear its opposite ;
The timorous stag starts from the thicket wild,
The fearful crane springs from the splashy fen,
The shining snake glides o'er the bending grass,
The stag turns head, and bays the crying hounds ;
The crane o'ertaken fighteth with the hawk ;
The snake doth turn, and bite the padding foot.
And if your Majesty's afraid of Philip,
You are more like a lion than a crane ;
Therefore I beg I may return to England.

KING.

Sir Thomas, now I understand your mirth,
Which often plays with wisdom for its pastime,
And brings good counsel from the breast of laughter.
I hope you'll stay and see us fight this battle,
And reap rich harvest in the fields of Cressy ;
Then go to England, tell them how we fight,
And set all hearts on fire to be with us.
Philip is plumed, and thinks we flee from him,
Else he would never dare to attack us.   Now,
Now the quarry's set ! and Death doth sport
In the bright sunshine of this fatal day.

DAGWORTH.

Now my heart dances, and I am as light
As the young bridegroom going to be married.
Now must I to my soldiers, get them ready,
Furbish our armours bright, new-plume our helms ;
And we will sing like the young housewives busied
In the dairy.   Now my feet are wing'd, but not
For flight, an please your grace.

KING.

If all my soldiers are as pleased as you,
'Twill be a gallant thing to fight or die ;
Then I can never be afraid of Philip.

DAGWORTH.

A raw-boned fellow t'other day passed by me ;
I told him to put off his hungry looks—
He answered me, " I hunger for another battle."
I saw a little Welshman with a fiery face.
I told him he looked like a candle half
Burned out : he answered, he was " pig enough
To light another pattle."   Last night, beneath
The moon I walked abroad, when all had pitched
Their tents, and all were still ;
I heard a blooming youth singing a song
He had composed, and at each pause he wiped
His dropping eyes.   The ditty was, " If he
Returned victorious, he should wed a maiden
Fairer than snow, and rich as midsummer."
Another wept, and wished health to his father.
I chid them both, but gave them noble hopes.
These are the minds that glory in the battle,
And leap and dance to hear the trumpet sound.

KING.

Sir Thomas Dagworth, be thou near our person ;
Thy heart is richer than the vales of France ;
I will not part with such a man as thee.
If Philip came armed in the ribs of death,
And shook his mortal dart against my head,
Thou'dst laugh his fury into nerveless shame !
Go now, for thou art suited to the work,
Throughout the camp ; inflame the timorous,
Blow up the sluggish into ardour, and
Confirm the strong with strength, the weak inspire,
And wing their brows with hope and expectation :
Then to our tent return, and meet to council.

[*Exit* DAGWORTH.

CHANDOS.

That man's a hero in his closet, and more
A hero to the servants of his house
Than to the gaping world ; he carries windows
In that enlargèd breast of his, that all
May see what's done within.

PRINCE.

He is a genuine Englishman, my Chandos,
And hath the spirit of Liberty within him.
Forgive my prejudice, Sir John ; I think
My Englishmen the bravest people on
The face of the earth.

CHANDOS.

Courage, my Lord, proceeds from self-dependence ;
Teach man to think he's a free agent,
Give but a slave his liberty, he'll shake

Off sloth, and build himself a hut, and hedge
A spot of ground ; this he'll defend ; 'tis his
By right of nature.   Thus set in action,
He will still move onward to plan conveniences,
Till glory fires his breast to enlarge his castle ;
While the poor slave drudges all day, in hope
To rest at night.

KING.

O Liberty, how glorious art thou !
I see thee hovering o'er my army, with
Thy wide-stretched plumes ; I see thee
Lead them on to battle ;
'I see thee blow thy golden trumpet while
Thy sons shout the strong shout of victory !
O noble Chandos, think thyself a gardener,
My son a vine, which I commit unto
Thy care.   Prune all extravagant shoots, and guide
The ambitious tendrils in the paths of wisdom ;
Water him with thy advice, and Heaven
Rain freshening dew upon his branches !   And,
O Edward, my dear son ! learn to think lowly of
Thyself, as we may all each prefer other—
Tis the best policy, and 'tis our duty.

[*Exit* KING EDWARD.

PRINCE.

And may our duty, Chandos, be our pleasure—
Now we are alone, Sir John, I will unburden
And breathe my hopes into the burning air,
Where thousand Deaths are posting up and down,
Commissioned to this fatal field of Cressy.

Methinks I see them arm my gallant soldiers,
And gird the sword upon each thigh, and fit
Each shining helm, and string each stubborn bow,
And dance to the neighing of our steeds.
Methinks the shout begins, the battle burns :
Methinks I see them perch on English crests,
And roar the wild flame of fierce war upon
The throngèd enemy !   In truth, I am too full ;
It is my sin to love the noise of war.
Chandos, thou seest my weakness ; strong Nature
Will bend or break us : my blood, like a springtide,
Does rise so high to overflow all bounds.
Of moderation ; while Reason, in her
Frail bark, can see no shore or bound for vast
Ambition.   Come, take the helm, my Chandos,
That my full-blown sails overset me not
In the wild tempest.   Condemn my 'ventrous youth
That plays with danger, as the innocent child,
Unthinking, plays upon the viper's den :
I am a coward in my reason, Chandos.

CHANDOS.

You are a man, my prince, and a brave man,
If I can judge of actions ; but your heat
Is the effect of youth, and want of use :
Use makes the armèd field and noisy war
Pass over as a summer cloud, unregarded,
Or but expected as a thing of course.
Age is contemplative ; each rolling year
Brings forth fruit to the mind's treasure-house :—
While vacant youth doth crave and seek about
Within itself, and findeth discontent,
Then, tired of thought, impatient takes the wing,

Seizes the fruits of time, attacks experience,
Roams round vast Nature's forest, where no bounds
Are set, the swiftest may have room, the strongest
Find prey ; till, tired at length, sated and tired
With the changing sameness, old variety,
We sit us down, and view our former joys
With distaste and dislike.

PRINCE.

Then if we must tug for experience,
Let us not fear to beat round Nature's wilds,
And rouse the strongest prey : then if we fall,
We fall with glory.   I know the wolf
Is dangerous to fight, not good for food,
Nor is the hide a comely vestment ; so
We have our battle for our pains.   I know
That youth has need of age to point fit prey,
And oft the stander-by shall steal the fruit
Of th' other's labour.   This is philosophy ;
These are the tricks of the world ; but the pure soul
Shall mount on native wings, disdaining
Little sport, and cut a path into the heaven of glory,
Leaving a track of light for men to wonder at.
I'm glad my father does not hear me talk ;
You can find friendly excuses for me, Chandos.
But do you not think, Sir John, that, if it please
Th' Almighty to stretch out my span of life,
I shall with pleasure view a glorious action
Which my youth mastered ?

CHANDOS.

Considerate age, my Lord, views motives,
And not acts ; when neither warbling voice
Nor trilling pipe is heard, nor pleasure sits

With trembling age, the voice of Conscience then,
Sweeter than music in a summer's eve,
Shall warble round the snowy head, and keep
Sweet symphony to feathered angels, sitting
As guardians round your chair ; then shall the pulse
Beat slow, and taste and touch, and sight, and sound,
    and smell,
That sing and dance round Reason's fine-wrought
    throne,
Shall flee away, and leave them all forlorn ;
Yet not forlorn if Conscience is his friend.

                                        [*Exeunt.*

SCENE, *in* Sir Thomas Dagworth's *Tent.*

DAGWORTH, *and* WILLIAM *his man.*

DAGWORTH.

Bring hither my armour, William.
Ambition is the growth of every clime.

WILLIAM.

Does it grow in England, sir ?

DAGWORTH.

Ay, it grows most in lands most cultivated.

WILLIAM.

Then it grows most in France ; the vines here
Are finer than any we have in England.

DAGWORTH.

Ay, but the oaks are not.

WILLIAM.

What is the tree you mentioned ?   I don't think
I ever saw it.

DAGWORTH.

Ambition.

WILLIAM.

Is it a little creeping root that grows in ditches ?

DAGWORTH.

Thou dost not understand me, William.
It is a root that grows in every breast ;
Ambition is the desire or passion that one man
Has to get before another, in any pursuit after glory;
But I don't think you have any of it.

WILLIAM.

Yes, I have ; I have a great ambition to know every-
thing, sir.

DAGWORTH.

But, when our first ideas are wrong, what follows
must all be wrong, of course : 'tis best to know a
little, and to know that little aright.

WILLIAM.

Then, sir, I should be glad to know if it was not
ambition that brought over our King to France to
fight for his right.

DAGWORTH.

Though the knowledge of that will not profit thee
much, yet I will tell you that it was ambition.

WILLIAM.

Then, if ambition is a sin, we are all guilty in coming with him, and in fighting for him.

DAGWORTH.

Now, William, thou dost thrust the question home ; but I must tell you that, guilt being an act of the mind, none are guilty but those whose minds are prompted by that same ambition.

WILLIAM.

Now, I always thought that a man might be guilty of doing wrong without knowing it was wrong.

DAGWORTH.

Thou art a natural philosopher, and knowest truth by instinct ; while reason runs aground, as we have run our argument. Only remember, William, all have it in their power to know the motives of their own actions, and 'tis a sin to act without some reason.

WILLIAM.

And whoever acts without reason may do a great deal of harm without knowing it.

DAGWORTH.

Thou art an endless moralist.

WILLIAM.

Now there's a story come into my head, that I will tell your honour, if you'll give me leave.

DAGWORTH.

No, William, save it till another time ; this is no time for story-telling. But here comes one who is as entertaining as a good story.

Enter PETER BLUNT.

PETER.

Yonder's a musician going to play before the King ; it's a new song about the French and English.   And the Prince has made the minstrel a squire, and given him I don't know what, and I can't tell whether he don't mention us all one by one ; and he is to write another about all us that are to die, that we may be remembered in Old England, for all our blood and bones are in France ;   and a great deal more that we shall all hear by and by.   And I came to tell your honour, because you love to hear war-songs.

DAGWORTH.

And who is this minstrel, Peter, dost know ?

PETER.

Oh ay, I forgot to tell that ;   he has got the same name as Sir John Chandos that the Prince is always with—the wise man that knows us all as well as your honour, only ain't so good-natured.

DAGWORTH.

I thank you, Peter, for your information, but not for your compliment, which is not true.   There's as much difference between him and me as between glittering sand and fruitful mould ;   or shining glass and a wrought diamond, set in rich gold, and fitted to the finger of an Emperor ;   such is that worthy Chandos.

PETER.

I know your honour does not think anything of yourself, but everybody else does.

DAGWORTH.

Go, Peter, get you gone ; flattery is delicious, even from the lips of a babbler.   *[Exit* PETER.

WILLIAM.

I never flatter your honour.

DAGWORTH.

I don't know that.

WILLIAM.

Why you know, sir, when we were in England, at the tournament at Windsor, and the Earl of Warwick was tumbled over, you asked me if he did not look well when he fell ; and I said no, he looked very foolish ; and you was very angry with me for not flattering you.

DAGWORTH.

You mean that I was angry with you for not flattering the Earl of Warwick.   *[Exeunt.*

SCENE, SIR THOMAS DAGWORTH'S *Tent.*

SIR THOMAS DAGWORTH. *To him enter* SIR WALTER MANNY.

SIR WALTER.

Sir Thomas Dagworth, I have been weeping
Over the men that are to die to-day.

DAGWORTH.

Why, brave Sir Walter, you or I may fall.

SIR WALTER.

I know this breathing flesh must lie and rot,
Covered with silence and forgetfulness.
Death wins in cities' smoke, and in still night,
When men sleep in their beds, walketh about.
How many in walled cities lie and groan,
Turning themselves upon their beds,
Talking with Death, answering his hard demands !
How many walk in darkness, terrors are round
The curtains of their beds, destruction is
Ready at the door !   How many sleep
In earth, covered with stones and deathy dust,
Resting in quietness whose spirits walk
Upon the clouds of heaven, to die no more !
Yet death is terrible, though borne on angels' wings.
How terrible then is the field of Death,
Where he doth rend the vault of heaven,
And shake the gates of hell !
O Dagworth, France is sick ! the very sky,
Though sunshine light it, seems to me as pale
As the pale fainting man on his death-bed,
Whose face is shown by light of sickly taper.
It makes me sad and sick at very heart ;
Thousands must fall to-day.

DAGWORTH.

Thousands of souls must leave this prison-house,
To be exalted to those heavenly fields
Where songs of triumph, palms of victory,
Where peace and joy and love and calm content,
Sit singing in the azure clouds, and strew
Flowers of heaven's growth over the banquet-table.

Bind ardent hope upon your feet like shoes,
Put on the robe of preparation !
The table is prepared in shining heaven,
The flowers of immortality are blown ;
Let those that fight fight in good steadfastness,
And those that fall shall rise in victory.

SIR WALTER.

I've often seen the burning field of war,
And often heard the dismal clang of arms ;
But never, till this fatal day of Cressy,
Has my soul fainted with these views of death.
I seem to be in one great charnel-house,
And seem to scent the rotten carcasses ;
I seem to hear the dismal yells of Death,
While the black gore drops from his horrid jaws:
Yet I not fear the monster in his pride—
But O ! the souls that are to die to-day !

DAGWORTH.

Stop, brave Sir Walter ; let me drop a tear,
Then let the clarion of war begin ;
I'll fight and weep, 'tis in my country's cause ;
I'll weep and shout for glorious liberty.
Grim war shall laugh and shout, decked in tears,
And blood shall flow like streams across the meadows,
That murmur down their pebbly channels, and
Spend their sweet lives to do their country service :
Then shall England's verdure shoot, her fields shall
    smile,
Her ships shall sing across the foaming sea,
Her mariners shall use the flute and viol,

And rattling guns, and black and dreary war,
Shall be no more.

SIR WALTER.

Well, let the trumpet sound, and the drum beat ;
Let war stain the blue heavens with bloody banners ;
I'll draw my sword, nor ever sheathe it up
Till England blow the trump of victory,
Or I lay stretched upon the field of death. [*Exeunt.*

SCENE, *In the Camp.*

*Several of the Warriors met at the King's Tent with a
Minstrel, who sings the following Song :*

O sons of Trojan Brutus clothed in war,
Whose voices are the thunder of the field,
Rolling dark clouds o'er France, muffling the sun
In sickly darkness like a dim eclipse,
Threatening as the red brow of storms, as fire
Burning up nations in your wrath and fury !

Your ancestors came from the fires of Troy
(Like lions roused by lightning from their dens,
Whose eyes do glare against the stormy fires),
Heated with war, filled with the blood of Greeks,
With helmets hewn, and shields covered with gore,
In navies black, broken with wind and tide :

They landed in firm array upon the rocks
Of Albion ; they kissed the rocky shore ;
" Be thou our mother and our nurse," they said ;

" Our children's mother, and thou shalt be our grave,
The sepulchre of ancient Troy, from whence
Shall rise cities, and thrones, and arms, and awful
    powers."

Our fathers swarm from the ships.   Giant voices
Are heard from the hills, the enormous sons
Of Ocean run from rocks and caves ; wild men,
Naked and roaring like lions, hurling rocks,
And wielding knotty clubs, like oaks entangled
Thick as a forest, ready for the axe.

Our fathers move in firm array to battle ;
The savage monsters rush like roaring fire ;
Like as a forest roars with crackling flames,
When the red lightning, borne by furious storms,
Lights on some woody shore ; the parchèd heavens
Rain fire into the molten raging sea.

The smoking trees are strewn upon the shore,
Spoiled of their verdure.   Oh how oft have they
Defied the storm that howlèd o'er their heads !
Our fathers, sweating, lean on their spears, and view
The mighty dead : giant bodies streaming blood,
Dread visages frowning in silent death.

Then Brutus spoke, inspired ; our fathers sit
Attentive on the melancholy shore:
Hear ye the voice of Brutus—" The flowing waves
Of time come rolling o'er my breast ", he said ;
" And my heart labours with futurity.
Our sons shall rule the empire of the sea.

" Their mighty wings shall stretch from East to West.
Their nest is in the sea, but they shall roam
Like eagles for the prey ; nor shall the young
Crave to be heard ; for plenty shall bring forth,
Cities shall sing, and vales in rich array
Shall laugh, whose fruitful laps bend down with ful-
　　ness.

" Our sons shall rise from thrones in joy,
Each one buckling on his armour ; Morning
Shall be prevented by their swords gleaming,
And Evening hear their song of victory :
Their towers shall be built upon the rocks,
Their daughters shall sing, surrounded with shining
　　spears.

" Liberty shall stand upon the cliffs of Albion,
Casting her blue eyes over the green ocean ;
Or tow'ring stand upon the roaring waves.
Stretching her mighty spear o'er distant lands ;
While with her eagle wings she covereth
Fair Albion's shore, and all her families."

SONGS OF INNOCENCE.

SONGS OF INNOCENCE.

INTRODUCTION.

PIPING down the valleys wild,
  Piping songs of pleasant glee,
On a cloud I saw a child,
  And he laughing said to me :

" Pipe a song about a Lamb ! "
  So I piped with merry cheer.
" Piper, pipe that song again ; "
  So I piped : he wept to hear.

" Drop thy pipe, thy happy pipe ;
  Sing thy songs of happy cheer ! "
So I sung the same again,
  While he wept with joy to hear.

" Piper, sit thee down and write
  In a book that all may read.
So he vanished from my sight :
  And I plucked a hollow reed.

And I made a rural pen,
  And I stained the water clear,
And I wrote my happy songs
  Every child may joy to hear.

THE SHEPHERD.

How sweet is the shepherd's sweet lot !
From the morn to the evening he strays ;
He shall follow his sheep all the day,
And his tongue shall be fillèd with praise.

For he hears the lambs' innocent call,
And he hears the ewes' tender reply ;
He is watchful while they are in peace,
For they know when their shepherd is nigh.

THE ECHOING GREEN.

The sun does arise,
And make happy the skies ;
The merry bells ring
To welcome the Spring ;
The skylark and thrush,
The birds of the bush,
Sing louder around
To the bells' cheerful sound ;
While our sports shall be seen
On the echoing green.

Old John, with white hair,
Does laugh away care,
Sitting under the oak,
Among the old folk.
They laugh at our play,
And soon they all say,
" Such, such were the joys
When we all—girls and boys—·
In our youth-time were seen
On the echoing green."

Till the little ones, weary,
No more can be merry :
The sun does descend,
And our sports have an end.
Round the laps of their mothers
Many sisters and brothers,
Like birds in their nest,
Are ready for rest,
And sport no more seen
On the darkening green.

THE LAMB.

LITTLE lamb, who made thee ?
Dost thou know who made thee,
Gave thee life, and bid thee feed
By the stream and o'er the mead ;
Gave thee clothing of delight,
Softest clothing, woolly, bright ;
Gave thee such a tender voice,
Making all the vales rejoice ?
   Little lamb, who made thee ?
   Dost thou know who made thee ?

Little lamb, I'll tell thee ;
Little lamb, I'll tell thee :
He is callèd by thy name,
For He calls Himself a Lamb.
He is meek, and He is mild,
He became a little child.
I a child, and thou a lamb,
We are callèd by his name.
   Little lamb, God bless thee !
   Little lamb, God bless thee !

THE LITTLE BLACK BOY.

My mother bore me in the southern wild,
    And I am black, but O my soul is white !
White as an angel is the English child,
    But I am black, as if bereaved of light.

My mother taught me underneath a tree,
    And, sitting down before the heat of day,
She took me on her lap and kissèd me,
    And, pointing to the East, began to say :

" Look on the rising sun : there God does live,
    And gives His light, and gives His heat away,
And flowers and trees and beasts and men receive
    Comfort in morning, joy in the noonday.

" And we are put on earth a little space,
    That we may learn to bear the beams of love ;
And these black bodies and this sunburnt face
    Are but a cloud, and like a shady grove.

" For, when our souls have learned the heat to bear,
    The cloud will vanish, we shall hear His voice,
Saying, ' Come out from the grove, my love and care,
    And round my golden tent like lambs rejoice.' "

Thus did my mother say, and kissèd me,
    And thus I say to little English boy.
When I from black, and he from white cloud free,
    And round the tent of God like lambs we joy,

I'll shade him from the heat till he can bear
    To lean in joy upon our Father's knee ;
And then I'll stand and stroke his silver hair,
    And be like him, and he will then love me.

THE BLOSSOM.

Merry, merry sparrow !
Under leaves so green
A happy blossom
Sees you, swift as arrow,
Seek your cradle narrow,
Near my bosom.
Pretty, pretty robin !
Under leaves so green
A happy blossom
Hears you sobbing, sobbing,
Pretty, pretty robin,
Near my bosom.

THE CHIMNEY-SWEEPER.

WHEN my mother died I was very young,
And my father sold me while yet my tongue
Could scarcely cry " Weep ! weep ! weep ! weep ! "
So your chimneys I sweep, and in soot I sleep.

There's little Tom Dacre, who cried when his head,
That curled like a lamb's back, was shaved ; so I said,
" Hush, Tom ! never mind it, for, when your head's
    bare,
You know that the soot cannot spoil your white hair."

And so he was quiet, and that very night,
As Tom was asleeping, he had such a sight !—
That thousands of sweepers, Dick, Joe, Ned, and Jack,
Were all of them locked up in coffins of black.

And by came an angel, who had a bright key,
And he opened the coffins, and set them all free ;
Then down a green plain, leaping, laughing, they run
And wash in a river, and shine in the sun.

Then naked and white, all their bags left behind,
They rise upon clouds, and sport in the wind ;
And the angel told Tom, if he'd be a good boy,
He'd have God for his father, and never want ; joy.

And so Tom awoke, and we rose in the dark,
And got with our bags and our brushes to work.
Though the morning was cold, Tom was happy and
    warm :
So, if all do their duty, they need not fear harm.

THE LITTLE BOY LOST.

" Father, father, where are you going ?
    O do not walk so fast !
Speak, father, speak to your little boy,
    Or else I shall be lost."

The night was dark, no father was there,
    The child was wet with dew ;
The mire was deep, and the child did weep,
    And away the vapour flew.

THE LITTLE BOY FOUND.

The little boy lost in the lonely fen,
    Led by the wandering light,
Began to cry, but God, ever nigh,
    Appeared like his father, in white.

He kissed the child, and by the hand led,
   And to his mother brought,
Who in sorrow pale, through the lonely dale,
   Her little boy weeping sought.

LAUGHING SONG.

WHEN the green woods laugh with the voice of joy,
And the dimpling stream runs laughing by ;
When the air does laugh with our merry wit,
And the green hill laughs with the noise of it ;

When the meadows laugh with lively green,
And the grasshopper laughs in the merry scene ;
When Mary and Susan and Emily
With their sweet round mouths sing " Ha ha he ! "

When the painted birds laugh in the shade,
Where our table with cherries and nuts is spread :
Come live, and be merry, and join with me,
To sing the sweet chorus of " Ha ha he ! "

A CRADLE SONG.

SWEET dreams, form a shade
O'er my lovely infant's head !
Sweet dreams of pleasant streams
By happy, silent, moony beams !

Sweet Sleep, with soft down
Weave thy brows an infant crown !
Sweet Sleep, angel mild,
Hover o'er my happy child !

Sweet smiles, in the night
Hover over my delight !
Sweet smiles, mother's smiles,
All the livelong night beguiles.

Sweet moans, dovelike sighs,
Chase not slumber from thine eyes !
Sweet moans, sweeter smiles,
All the dovelike moans beguiles.

Sleep, sleep, happy child !
All creation slept and smiled.
Sleep, sleep, happy sleep,
While o'er thee thy mother weep.

Sweet babe, in thy face
Holy image I can trace ;
Sweet babe, once like thee
Thy Maker lay, and wept for me :

Wept for me, for thee, for all,
When He was an infant small.
Thou His image ever see,
Heavenly face that smiles on thee

Smiles on thee, on me, on all,
Who became an infant small ;
Infant smiles are his own smiles ;
Heaven and earth to peace beguiles.

THE DIVINE IMAGE.

To Mercy, Pity, Peace, and Love,
   All pray in their distress,
And to these virtues of delight
   Return their thankfulness.

For Mercy, Pity, Peace, and Love,
   Is God our Father dear ;
And Mercy, Pity, Peace, and Love,
   Is man, His child and care.

For Mercy has a human heart ;
   Pity, a human face ;
And Love, the human form divine :
   And Peace, the human dress.

Then every man, of every clime,
   That prays in his distress,
Prays to the human form divine :
   Love, Mercy, Pity, Peace.

And all must love the human form,
   In heathen, Turk, or Jew.
Where Mercy, Love, and Pity dwell,
   There God is dwelling too.

HOLY THURSDAY.

'Twas on a holy Thursday, their innocent faces clean,
The children walking two and two, in red, and blue, and
   green :
Grey-headed beadles walked before, with wands as
   white as snow,
Till into the high dome of Paul's they like Thames
   waters flow.

O what a multitude they seemed, these flowers of Lon-
   don town !
Seated in companies they sit, with radiance all their
   own.

The hum of multitudes was there, but multitudes of
    lambs,
Thousands of little boys and girls raising their innocent
    hands.

Now like a mighty wind they raise to heaven the voice
    of song,
Or like harmonious thunderings the seats of heaven
    among :
Beneath them sit the aged men, wise guardians of the
    poor.
Then cherish pity, lest you drive an angel from your
    door.

NIGHT.

THE sun descending in the West,
The evening star does shine ;
The birds are silent in their nest,
And I must seek for mine.
    The moon, like a flower
    In heaven's high bower,
    With silent delight,
    Sits and smiles on the night.

Farewell, green fields and happy groves,
Where flocks have took delight.
Where lambs have nibbled, silent moves
The feet of angels bright ;
    Unseen, they pour blessing,
    And joy without ceasing,
    On each bud and blossom,
    And each sleeping bosom.

They look in every thoughtless nest
Where birds are covered warm ;
They visit caves of every beast,
To keep them all from harm :
    If they see any weeping
    That should have been sleeping,
    They pour sleep on their head,
    And sit down by their bed.

When wolves and tigers howl for prey
They pitying stand and weep ;
Seeking to drive their thirst away,
And keep them from the sheep.
    But, if they rush dreadful,
    The angels, most heedful,
    Receive each mild spirit,
    New worlds to inherit.

And there the lion's ruddy eyes
Shall flow with tears of gold :
And pitying the tender cries,
And walking round the fold :
    Saying : " Wrath by His meekness,
    And, by His health, sickness,
    Is driven away
    From our immortal day.

" And now beside thee, bleating lamb,
I can lie down and sleep,
Or think on Him who bore thy name,
Graze after thee, and weep.
    For, washed in life's river,
    My bright mane for ever
    Shall shine like the gold,
    As I guard o'er the fold."

SPRING.

Sound the flute !
Now it 's mute !
Birds delight,
Day and night,
Nightingale,
In the dale,
Lark in sky,—
Merrily,
Merrily, merrily to welcome in the year.

Little boy,
Full of joy,
Little girl,
Sweet and small ;
Cock does crow,
So do you ;
Merry voice,
Infant noise ;
Merrily, merrily we welcome in the year.

Little lamb,
Here I am ;
Come and lick
My white neck ;
Let me pull
Your soft wool ;
Let me kiss
Your soft face ;
Merrily, merrily we welcome in the year.

NURSE'S SONG.

WHEN the voices of children are heard on the green,
  And laughing is heard on the hill,
My heart is at rest within my breast,
  And everything else is still.
" Then come home, my children, the sun is gone down,
  And the dews of night arise ;
Come, come, leave off play, and let us away,
  Till the morning appears in the skies."

" No, no, let us play, for it is yet day,
  And we cannot go to sleep ;
Besides, in the sky the little birds fly,
  And the hills are all covered with sheep."
" Well, well, go and play till the light fades away,
  And then go home to bed."
The little ones leaped, and shouted, and laughed,
  And all the hills echoèd.

INFANT JOY.

" I have no name ;
I am but two days old."
What shall I call thee ?
" I happy am,
Joy is my name."
Sweet joy befall thee !

Pretty joy !
Sweet joy but two days old.
Sweet joy I call thee :
Thou dost smile,
I sing the while ;
Sweet joy befall thee !

A DREAM.

Once a dream did weave a shade
O'er my angel-guarded bed,
That an emmet lost its way
Where on grass methought I lay.

Troubled, wildered and forlorn,
Dark, benighted, travel-worn,
Over many a tangled spray,
All heart-broke, I heard her say :

" O my children ! do they cry,
Do they hear their father sigh ?
Now they look abroad to see,
Now return and weep for me."

Pitying, I dropped a tear :
But I saw a glow-worm near,
Who replied, " What wailing wight
Calls the watchman of the night ?

" I am set to light the ground,
While the beetle goes his round !
Follow now the beetle's hum ;
Little wanderer, hie thee home ! "

ON ANOTHER'S SORROW.

CAN I see another's woe,
And not be in sorrow too?
Can I see another's grief,
And not seek for kind relief?

Can I see a falling tear,
And not feel my sorrow's share?
Can a father see his child
Weep, nor be with sorrow filled?

Can a mother sit and hear
An infant groan, an infant fear?
No, no! never can it be!
Never, never can it be!

And can He who smiles on all
Hear the wren with sorrows small,
Hear the small bird's grief and care,
Hear the woes that infants bear—

And not sit beside the nest,
Pouring pity in their breast,
And not sit the cradle near,
Weeping tear on infant's tear?

And not sit both night and day,
Wiping all our tears away?
O no! never can it be!
Never, never can it be!

He doth give His joy to all:
He becomes an infant small,
He becomes a man of woe,
He doth feel the sorrow too.

Think not thou canst sigh a sigh,
And thy Maker is not by :
Think not thou canst weep a tear,
And thy Maker is not near.

O He gives to us His joy,
That our grief He may destroy :
Till our grief is fled and gone
He doth sit by us and moan.

SONGS OF EXPERIENCE.

SONGS OF EXPERIENCE.

INTRODUCTION.

HEAR the voice of the Bard,
Who present, past, and future, sees ;
Whose ears have heard
The Holy Word
That walked among the ancient trees ;

Calling the lapsèd soul,
And weeping in the evening dew ;
That might control
The starry pole,
And fallen, fallen light renew !

" O Earth, O Earth, return !
Arise from out the dewy grass !
Night is worn,
And the morn
Rises from the slumbrous mass.

" Turn away no more ;
Why wilt thou turn away ?
The starry floor.
The watery shore,
Is given thee till the break of day."

EARTH'S ANSWER.

EARTH raised up her head
From the darkness dread and drear,
Her light fled,
Stony, dread,
And her locks covered with grey despair.

" Prisoned on watery shore,
Starry jealousy does keep my den
Cold and hoar ;
Weeping o'er,
I hear the father of the ancient men.

" Selfish father of men !
Cruel, jealous, selfish fear !
Can delight,
Chained in night,
The virgins of youth and morning bear ?

" Does spring hide its joy,
When buds and blossoms grow ?
Does the sower
Sow by night,
Or the ploughman in darkness plough ?

" Break this heavy chain,
That does freeze my bones around !
Selfish, vain,
Eternal bane,
That free love with bondage bound."

THE CLOD AND THE PEBBLE.

" Love seeketh not itself to please,
    Nor for itself hath any care,
But for another gives its ease,
    And builds a heaven in hell's despair."

So sung a little clod of clay,
    Trodden with the cattle's feet,
But a pebble of the brook
    Warbled out these metres meet :

" Love seeketh only Self to please,
    To bind another to its delight,
Joys in another's loss of ease,
    And builds a hell in heaven's despite."

HOLY THURSDAY.

Is this a holy thing to see
    In a rich and fruitful land,—
Babes reduced to misery,
    Fed with cold and usurous hand ?

Is that trembling cry a song ?
    Can it be a song of joy ?
And so many children poor ?
    It is a land of poverty !

And their sun does never shine,
    And their fields are bleak and bare,
And their ways are filled with thorns,
    It is eternal winter there.

For where'er the sun does shine,
　And where'er the rain does fall,
Babe can never hunger there,
　Nor poverty the mind appal.

THE LITTLE GIRL LOST.

In futurity
I prophesy
That the earth from sleep
(Grave the sentence deep)

Shall arise, and seek
For her maker meek ;
And the desert wild
Become a garden mild.

In the southern clime,
Where the summer's prime
Never fades away,
Lovely Lyca lay.

Seven summers old
Lovely Lyca told.
She had wandered long,
Hearing wild birds' song.

" Sweet sleep, come to me,
Underneath this tree ;
Do father, mother weep ?
Where can Lyca sleep ?

" Lost in desert wild
Is your little child.
How can Lyca sleep
If her mother weep ?

" If her heart does ache,
Then let Lyca wake
If my mother sleep,
Lyca shall not weep.

" Frowning, frowning night,
O'er this desert bright
Let thy moon arise,
While I close my eyes.

Sleeping Lyca lay,
While the beasts of prey,
Come from caverns deep,
Viewed the maid asleep.

The kingly lion stood,
And the virgin viewed :
Then he gambolled round
O'er the hallowed ground.

Leopards, tigers, play
Round her as she lay ;
While the lion old
Bowed his mane of gold,

And her bosom lick,
And upon her neck,
From his eyes of flame,
Ruby tears there came ;

While the lioness
Loosed her slender dress.
And naked they conveyed
To caves the sleeping maid.

THE LITTLE GIRL FOUND.

ALL the night in woe
Lyca's parents go
Over valleys deep,
While the deserts weep.

Tired and woe-begone,
Hoarse with making moan,
Arm in arm, seven days
They traced the desert ways.

Seven nights they sleep
Among shadows deep,
And dream they see their child
Starved in desert wild.

Pale through pathless ways
The fancied image strays,
Famished, weeping, weak,
With hollow piteous shriek.

Rising from unrest,
The trembling woman pressed
With feet of weary woe ;
She could no further go,

In his arms he bore
Her, armed with sorrow sore ;
Till before their way
A couching lion lay.

Turning back was vain :
Soon his heavy mane
Bore them to the ground,
Then he stalked around,

Smelling to his prey ;
But their fears allay
When he licks their hands,
And silent by them stands.

They look upon his eyes,
Filled with deep surprise ;
And wondering behold
A spirit armed in gold.

On his head a crown,
On his shoulders down
Flowed his golden hair.
Gone was all their care.

" Follow me ", he said ;
" Weep not for the maid ;
In my palace deep,
Lyca lies asleep."

Then they followèd
Where the vision led,
And saw their sleeping child
Among tigers wild.

To this day they dwell
In a lonely dell,
Nor fear the wolvish howl
Nor the lion's growl.

THE CHIMNEY-SWEEPER.

A LITTLE black thing among the snow,
Crying " weep ! weep ! " in notes of woe !
" Where are thy father and mother ?   Say ! "—
" They are both gone up to the church to pray.

" Because I was happy upon the heath,
And smiled among the winter's snow,
They clothed me in the clothes of death,
And taught me to sing the notes of woe.

" And because I am happy and dance and sing,
They think they have done me no injury,
And are gone to praise God and His priest and king,
Who make up a heaven of our misery."

NURSE'S SONG.

WHEN the voices of children are heard on the green,
    And whisperings are in the dale,
The days of my youth rise fresh in my mind,
    My face turns green and pale.

Then come home my children, the sun is gone down,
    And the dews of night arise ;
Your spring and your day are wasted in play,
    And your winter and night in disguise.

THE SICK ROSE.

O ROSE, thou art sick !
    The invisible worm,
That flies in the night,
    In the howling storm,

Has found out thy bed
    Of crimson joy,
And his dark secret love
    Does thy life destroy.

THE FLY.

LITTLE Fly,
Thy summer's play
My thoughtless hand
Has brushed away.

Am not I
A fly like thee ?
Or art not thou
A man like me ?

For I dance,
And drink, and sing,
Till some blind hand
Shall brush my wing.

If thought is life
And strength and breath,
And the want
Of thought is death ;

Then am I
A happy fly.
If I live,
Or if I die.

THE ANGEL.

I DREAMT a dream !   What can it mean ?
And that I was a maiden Queen
Guarded by an Angel mild :
Witless woe was ne'er beguiled !

And I wept both night and day,
And he wiped my tears away ;
And I wept both day and night,
And hid from him my heart's delight.

So he took his wings, and fled ;
Then the morn blushed rosy red.
I dried my tears, and armed my fears
With ten thousand shields and spears.

Soon my Angel came again ;
I was armed, he came in vain ;
For the time of youth was fled,
And grey hairs were on my head.

THE TIGER.

TIGER, tiger, burning bright
In the forests of the night,
What immortal hand or eye
Could frame thy fearful symmetry ?

In what distant deeps or skies
Burnt the fire of thine eyes ?
On what wings dare he aspire ?
What the hand dare seize the fire ?

And what shoulder and what art
Could twist the sinews of thy heart ?
And, when thy heart began to beat,
What dread hand and what dread feet ?

What the hammer ? what the chain ?
In what furnace was thy brain ?
What the anvil ? what dread grasp
Dare its deadly terrors clasp ?

When the stars threw down their spears
And watered heaven with their tears,
Did He smile His work to see ?
Did He who made the lamb make thee ?

Tiger, tiger, burning bright
In the forests of the night,
What immortal hand or eye
Dare frame thy fearful symmetry ?

MY PRETTY ROSE TREE.

A FLOWER was offered to me,
   Such a flower as May never bore ;
But I said, " I've a pretty rose tree,"
   And I passed the sweet flower o'er.

Then I went to my pretty rose tree,
   To tend her by day and by night ;
But my rose turned away with jealousy,
   And her thorns were my only delight.

AH, SUNFLOWER.

AH, Sunflower, weary of time,
   Who countest the steps of the sun ;
Seeking after that sweet golden clime
   Where the traveller's journey is done ;

Where the Youth pined away with desire,
   And the pale virgin shrouded in snow,
Arise from their graves, and aspire
   Where my Sunflower wishes to go !

THE LILY.

THE modest Rose puts forth a thorn,
The humble sheep a threat'ning horn :
While the Lily white shall in love delight,
Nor a thorn nor a threat stain her beauty bright.

THE GARDEN OF LOVE.

I WENT to the Garden of Love,
  And saw what I never had seen ;
A Chapel was built in the midst,
  Where I used to play on the green.

And the gates of this Chapel were shut,
  And " Thou shalt not " writ over the door ;
So I turned to the Garden of Love
  That so many sweet flowers bore.

And I saw it was filled with graves,
  And tombstones where flowers should be ;
And priests in black gowns were walking their rounds,
  And binding with briars my joys and desires.

THE LITTLE VAGABOND.

DEAR mother, dear mother, the Church is cold ;
But the Alehouse is healthy, and pleasant, and warm,
Besides, I can tell where I am used well ;
Such usage in heaven will never do well.

But, if at the Church they would give us some ale,
And a pleasant fire our souls to regale,
We'd sing and we'd pray all the livelong day,
Nor ever once wish from the Church to stray.

Then the Parson might preach, and drink, and sing,
And we'd be as happy as birds in the spring ;
And modest Dame Lurch, who is always at Church,
Would not have bandy children, nor fasting, nor
    birch.

And God, like a father, rejoicing to see
His children as pleasant and happy as He,
Would have no more quarrel with the Devil or the
    barrel,
But kiss him, and give him both drink and apparel.

LONDON.

I WANDER through each chartered street,
    Near where the chartered Thames does flow,
A mark in every face I meet,
    Marks of weakness, marks of woe.

In every cry of every man,
    In every infant's cry of fear,
In every voice, in every ban,
    The mind-forged manacles I hear :

How the chimney-sweeper's cry
    Every blackening church appals,
And the hapless soldier's sigh
    Runs in blood down palace-walls.

But most, through midnight streets I hear
    How the youthful harlot's curse
Blasts the new-born infant's tear,
    And blights with plagues the marriage-hearse.

THE HUMAN ABSTRACT.

PITY would be no more
If we did not make somebody poor,
And Mercy no more could be
If all were as happy as we.

And mutual fear brings Peace,
Till the selfish loves increase ;
Then Cruelty knits a snare,
And spreads his baits with care.

He sits down with holy fears,
And waters the ground with tears ;
Then Humility takes its root
Underneath his foot.

Soon spreads the dismal shade
Of Mystery over his head,
And the caterpillar and fly
Feed on the Mystery.

And it bears the fruit of Deceit,
Ruddy and sweet to eat,
And the raven his nest has made
In its thickest shade.

The gods of the earth and sea
Sought through nature to find this tree,
But their search was all in vain :
There grows one in the human Brain.

INFANT SORROW

My mother groaned, my father wept :
Into the dangerous world I leapt,
Helpless, naked, piping loud,
Like a fiend hid in a cloud.

Struggling in my father's hands,
Striving against my swaddling bands,
Bound and weary, I thought best
To sulk upon my mother's breast.

A POISON TREE

I was angry with my friend :
I told my wrath, my wrath did end.
I was angry with my foe :
I told it not, my wrath did grow.

And I watered it in fears
Night and morning with my tears,
And I sunnèd it with smiles
And with soft deceitful wiles.

And it grew both day and night,
Till it bore an apple bright,
And my foe beheld it shine,
And he knew that it was mine,—

And into my garden stole
When the night had veiled the pole ;
In the morning, glad, I see
My foe outstretched beneath the tree.

A LITTLE BOY LOST

" Nought loves another as itself,
      Nor venerates another so,
Nor is it possible to thought
      A greater than itself to know.

" And, father, how can I love you
      Or any of my brothers more ?
I love you like the little bird
      That picks up crumbs around the door."

The Priest sat by and heard the child ;
      In trembling zeal he seized his hair,
He led him by his little coat,
      And all admired the priestly care.

And standing on the altar high,
      " Lo, what a fiend is here ! " said he :
" One who sets reason up for judge
      Of our most holy mystery."

The weeping child could not be heard,
      The weeping parents wept in vain :
They stripped him to his little shirt,
      And bound him in an iron chain,

And burned him in a holy place
      Where many had been burned before ;
The weeping parents wept in vain.
      Are such things done on Albion's shore ?

A LITTLE GIRL LOST

CHILDREN of the future age,
Reading this indignant page,
Know that in a former time
Love, sweet love, was thought a crime.

In the age of gold,
Free from winter's cold,
Youth and maiden bright,
To the holy light,
Naked in the sunny beams delight.

Once a youthful pair,
Filled with softest care,
Met in garden bright
Where the holy light.
Had just removed the curtains of the night.

There, in rising day
On the grass they play ;
Parents were afar,
Strangers came not near,
And the maiden soon forgot her fear.

Tired with kisses sweet,
They agree to meet
When the silent sleep
Waves o'er heaven's deep,
And the weary tired wanderers weep.

To her father white
Came the maiden bright ;
But his loving look,
Like the holy book,
All her tender limbs with terror shook.

" Ona, pale and weak,
To thy father speak !
O the trembling fear !
O the dismal care
That shakes the blossoms of my hoary hair ! "

A DIVINE IMAGE.

CRUELTY has a human heart,
　　And Jealousy a human face ;
Terror the human form divine,
　　And Secrecy the human dress.

The human dress is forgèd iron,
　　The human form a fiery forge,
The human face a furnace sealed,
　　The human heart its hungry gorge.

A CRADLE SONG

SLEEP, sleep, beauty bright,
Dreaming in the joys of night ;
Sleep, sleep ; in thy sleep
Little sorrows sit and weep.

Sweet babe, in thy face
Soft desires I can trace,
Secret joys and secret smiles,
Little pretty infant wiles.

As thy softest limbs I feel,
Smiles as of the morning steal
O'er thy cheek, and o'er thy breast
Where thy little heart doth rest.

O the cunning wiles that creep
In thy little heart asleep !
When thy little heart doth wake,
Then the dreadful light shall break.

THE SCHOOLBOY.

I LOVE to rise in a summer morn,
  When the birds sing on every tree :
The distant huntsman winds his horn,
  And the skylark sings with me ;
  O what sweet company !

But to go to school in a summer morn,—
  O it drives all joy away !
Under a cruel eye outworn,
  The little ones spend the day
  In sighing and dismay.

Ah then at times I drooping sit,
  And spend many an anxious hour ;
Nor in my book can I take delight,
  Nor sit in learning's bower,
  Worn through with the dreary shower.

How can the bird that is born for joy
  Sit in a cage and sing ?
How can a child when fears annoy,
  But droop his tender wing,
  And forget his youthful spring ?

O father and mother, if buds are nipped,
  And blossoms blown away ;
And if the tender plants are stripped
  Of their joy in the springing day,
  By sorrow and care's dismay,—

How shall the summer arise in joy,
  Or the summer fruits appear ?
Or how shall we gather what griefs destroy,
  Or bless the mellowing year,
  When the blasts of winter appear ?

TO TIRZAH.

WHATE'ER is born of mortal birth
Must be consumèd with the earth,
To rise from generation free :
Then what have I to do with thee ?

The sexes sprung from shame and pride,
Blowed in the morn, in evening died ;
But mercy changed death into sleep ;
The sexes rose to work and weep.

Thou, mother of my mortal part,
With cruelty didst mould my heart,
And with false self-deceiving tears
Didst blind my nostrils, eyes, and ears,

Didst close my tongue in senseless clay,
And me to mortal life betray.
The death of Jesus set me free :
Then what have I to do with thee ?

THE VOICE OF THE ANCIENT BARD.

YOUTH of delight ! come hither
And see the opening morn,
Image of Truth new-born.
Doubt is fled, and clouds of reason,
Dark disputes and artful teazing.
Folly is an endless maze ;
Tangled roots perplex her ways ;
How many have fallen there !
They stumble all night over bones of the dead ;
And feel—they know not what but care ;
And· wish to lead others, when they should be led.

IDEAS OF GOOD AND EVIL.

IDEAS OF GOOD AND EVIL.

DAYBREAK.

To find the western path,
Right through the gates of wrath
  I urge my way;
Sweet morning leads me on;
With soft repentant moan
  I see the break of day.

The war of swords and spears,
Melted by dewy tears,
  Exhales on high;
The sun is freed from fears,
And with soft grateful tears
  Ascends the sky.

THE WILD FLOWER'S SONG.

As I wandered in the forest
  The green leaves among,
I heard a wild flower
  Singing a song.

"I slept in the earth
  In the silent night;
I murmured my thoughts,
  And I felt delight.

" In the morning I went,
　As rosy as morn,
To seek for new joy,
　But I met with scorn."

AUGURIES OF INNOCENCE.

To see the world in a grain of sand,
　And a heaven in a wild flower ;
Hold infinity in the palm of your hand,
　And eternity in an hour.

YOUNG LOVE.

ARE not the joys of morning sweeter
　Than the joys of night ?
And are the vigorous joys of youth
　Ashamèd of the light ?

Let age and sickness silent rob
　The vineyard in the night ;
But those who burn with vigorous youth
　Pluck fruits before the light ?

THE BIRDS.

HE.

WHERE thou dwellest, in what grove,
Tell me, fair one, tell me, love ;
Where thou thy charming nest dost build.
O thou pride of every field !

SHE.

Yonder stands a lonely tree :
There I live and mourn for thee.
Morning drinks my silent tear,
And evening winds my sorrow bear.

HE.

O thou summer's harmony,
I have lived and mourned for thee ;
Each day I moan along the wood,
And night hath heard my sorrows loud.

SHE.

Dost thou truly long for me ?
And am I thus sweet to thee ?
Sorrow now is at an end,
O my lover and my friend !

HE.

Come ! on wings of joy we'll fly
To where my bower is hung on high ;
Come, and make thy calm retreat
Among green leaves and blossoms sweet.

THE LAND OF DREAMS.

AWAKE, awake, my little boy !
Thou wast thy mother's only joy.
Why dost thou weep in thy gentle sleep ?
Awake ! thy father doth thee keep.

" O what land is the land of dreams ?
What are its mountains and what are its streams ? "
" O father ! I saw my mother there,
Among the lilies by waters fair.

" Among the lambs clothèd in white,
She walked with her Thomas in sweet delight.
I wept for joy, like a dove I mourn—
O when shall I again return ? "

" Dear child ! I also by pleasant streams
Have wandered all night in the land of dreams ;
But, though calm and warm the waters wide,
I could not get to the other side."

" Father, O father ! what do we here,
In this land of unbelief and fear ?
The land of dreams is better far,
Above the light of the morning star."

TO MR. BUTTS.

To my friend Butts I write
My first vision of light,
On the yellow sands sitting.
The sun was emitting
His glorious beams
From heaven's high streams.
Over sea, over land,
My eyes did expand
Into regions of air,
Away from all care ;
Into regions of fire,
Remote from desire ;

The light of the morning
Heaven's mountains adorning.
In particles bright,
The jewels of light
Distinct shone and clear.
Amazed and in fear
I each particle gazed,
Astonished, amazed ;
For each was a man
Human-formed.   Swift I ran.
For they beckoned to me,
Remote by the sea,
Saying : " Each grain of sand,
Every stone on the land,
Each rock and each hill,
Each fountain and rill,
Each herb and each tree,
Mountain, hill, earth, and sea,
Cloud, meteor, and star,
Are men seen afar."
I stood in the streams
Of heaven's bright beams,
And saw Felpham sweet
Beneath my bright feet,
In soft female charms ;
And in her fair arms
My shadow I knew,
And my wife's shadow too,
And my sister and friend.
We like infants descend
In our shadows on earth,
Like a weak mortal birth.
My eyes more and more,

Like a sea without shore,
Continue expanding,
The heavens commanding,
Till the jewels of light,
Heavenly men beaming bright,
Appeared as one man,
Who complacent began
My limbs to enfold
In his beams of bright gold ;
Like dross purged away
All my mire and my clay.
Soft consumed in delight,
In his bosom sun-bright
I remained.   Soft he smiled,
And I heard his voice mild,
Saying : " This is my fold,
O thou ram horned with gold,
Who awakest from sleep
On the sides of the deep.
On the mountains around
The roarings resound
Of the lion and wolf,
The loud sea and deep gulf.
These are guards of my fold,
O thou ram horned with gold."
And the voice faded mild,——
I remained as a child ;
All I ever had known,
Before me bright shone ;
I saw you and your wife
By the fountains of life.
Such a vision to me
Appeared on the sea.

TO MY DEAR FRIEND, MRS. ANNA FLAXMAN.

THIS song to the flower of Flaxman's joy ;
To the blossom of hope, for a sweet decoy ;
Do all that you can, or all that you may,
To entice him to Felpham and far away.

Away to sweet Felpham, for heaven is there,
The ladder of angels descends through the air ;
On the turret its spiral does softly descend,
Through the village then winds, at my cot it does end.

You stand in the village and look up to heaven ;
The precious stones glitter on flight Seventy-seven ;
And my brother is there ; and my friend and thine
Descend and ascend with the bread and the wine.

The bread of sweet thought and the wine of delight
Feed the village of Felpham by day and by night ;
And at his own door the bless'd hermit does stand,
Dispensing, unceasing, to all the wide land.

THE PILGRIM

PHŒBE dressed like beauty's queen,
Jellicoe in faint pea-green,
Sitting all beneath a grot,
Where the little lambkins trot.

Maidens dancing ;—lovers sporting ;
All the country folk a-courting,
Susan, Johnny, Bob and Joe,
Lightly tripping on a row.

Happy people, who can be
In happiness compared to ye ?
The Pilgrim with his crook and hat,
Sees your happiness complete.

PROVERBS.

A ROBIN Redbreast in a cage
Puts all heaven in a rage ;
A dove-house filled with doves and pigeons
Shudders hell through all its regions.
A dog starved at his master's gate
Predicts the ruin of the state ;
A game-cock clipped and armed for fight
Doth the rising sun affright ;
A horse misused upon the road
Calls to heaven for human blood.
Every wolf's and lion's howl
Raises from hell a human soul ;
Each outcry of the hunted hare
A fibre from the brain does tear ;
A skylark wounded on the wing
Doth make a cherub cease to sing.

He who shall hurt the little wren
Shall never be beloved by men ;
He who the ox to wrath has moved
Shall never be by woman loved ;
He who shall train the horse to war
Shall never pass the Polar Bar.
The wanton boy that kills the fly
Shall feel the spider's enmity ;
He who torments the chafer's sprite.

Weaves a bower in endless night.
The caterpillar on the leaf
Repeats to thee thy mother's grief ;
The wild deer wandering here and there
Keep the human soul from care ;
The lamb misused breeds public strife,
And yet forgives the butcher's knife.
Kill not the moth nor butterfly,
For the last judgment draweth nigh ;
The beggar's dog and widow's cat,
Feed them and thou shalt grow fat.
Every tear from every eye
Becomes a babe in eternity ;
The bleat, the bark, bellow, and roar,
Are waves that beat on heaven's shore.

The bat that flits at close of eve
Has left the brain that won't believe ;
The owl that calls upon the night
Speaks the unbeliever's fright ;
The gnat that sings his summer's song
Poison gets from Slander's tongue ;
The poison of the snake and newt
Is the sweat of Envy's foot ;
The poison of the honey-bee
Is the artist's jealousy ;
The strongest poison ever known
Came from Cæsar's laurel crown.

Nought can deform the human race
Like to the armourer's iron brace ;
The soldier armed with sword and gun
Palsied strikes the summer's sun.

When gold and gems adorn the plough,
To peaceful arts shall Envy bow.
The beggar's rags fluttering in air
Do to rags the heavens tear ;
The prince's robes and beggar's rags
Are toadstools on the miser's bags.

One mite wrung from the labourer's hands
Shall buy and sell the miser's lands,
Or, if protected from on high,
Shall that whole nation sell and buy ;
The poor man's farthing is worth more
Than all the gold on Afric's shore.
The whore and gambler, by the state
Licensed, build that nation's fate ;
The harlot's cry from street to street
Shall weave Old England's winding sheet ;
The winner's shout, the loser's curse,
Shall dance before dead England's hearse.

He who mocks the infant's faith
Shall be mocked in age and death ;
He who shall teach the child to doubt
The rotting grave shall ne'er get out ;
He who respects the infant's faith
Triumphs over hell and death.
The babe is more than swaddling-bands
Throughout all these human lands ;
Tools were made, and born were hands,
Every farmer understands.

The questioner who sits so sly
Shall never know how to reply ;

He who replies to words of doubt
Doth put the light of knowledge out ;
A riddle, or the cricket's cry,
Is to doubt a fit reply.
The child's toys and the old man's reasons
Are the fruits of the two seasons.
The emmet's inch and eagle's mile
Make lame philosophy to smile.
A truth that's told with bad intent
Beats all the lies you can invent.
He who doubts from what he sees
Will ne'er believe, do what you please ;
If the sun and moon should doubt,
They'd immediately go out.

Every night and every morn
Some to misery are born ;
Every morn and every night
Some are born to sweet delight ;
Some are born to sweet delight,
Some are born to endless night.
Joy and woe are woven fine,
A clothing for the soul divine ;
Under every grief and pine
Runs a joy with silken twine.
It is right it should be so ;
Man was made for joy and woe ;
And, when this we rightly know,
Safely through the world we go.

We are led to believe a lie
When we see *with* not *through* the eye,
Which was born in a night to perish in a night
When the soul slept in beams of light.

God appears, and God is light
To those poor souls who dwell in night,
But doth a human form display
To those who dwell in realms of day.

THE GATES OF PARADISE

INTRODUCTION.

MUTUAL forgiveness of each vice,
Such are the Gates of Paradise,
Against the Accuser's chief desire,
Who walked among the stones of fire.
Jehovah's fingers wrote the Law :
He wept ; then rose in zeal and awe,
And, in the midst of Sinai's heat,
Hid it beneath His Mercy-seat.
   O Christians ! Christians ! tell me why
You rear it on your altars high !

THE KEYS OF THE GATES.

THE caterpillar on the leaf
Reminds thee of thy mother's grief.
My Eternal Man set in repose,
The Female from his darkness rose ;
And she found me beneath a tree,
A mandrake, and in her veil hid me.
Serpent reasonings us entice
Of good and evil, virtue, vice.
Doubt self-jealous, watery folly,

Struggling through Earth's melancholy.
Naked in air, in shame and fear,
Blind in fire, with shield and spear,
Two horrid reasoning cloven fictions.
In doubt which is self-contradiction,
A dark hermaphrodite I stood,—
Rational truth, root of evil and good.
Round me, flew the flaming sword ;
Round her, snowy whirlwinds roared,
Freezing her veil, the mundane shell.
I rent the veil where the dead dwell :
When weary man enters his cave,
He meets his Saviour in the grave.
Some find a female garment there,
And some a male, woven with care,
Lest the sexual garments sweet
Should grow a devouring winding-sheet.
One dies ! alas ! the living and dead !
One is slain, and one is fled !
In vain-glory hatched and nursed,
By double spectres, self-accursed.
My son ! my son ! thou treatest me
But as I have instructed thee.
On the shadows of the moon,
Climbing through night's highest noon :
In Time's ocean falling, drowned :
In aged ignorance profound,
Holy and cold, I clipped the wings
Of all sublunary things :
And in depths of icy dungeons
Closed the father and the sons,
But, when once I did descry
The Immortal Man that cannot die

Through evening shades I haste away
To close the labours of my day.
The door of Death I open found,
And the worm weaving in the ground :
Thou'rt my mother, from the womb ;
Wife, sister, daughter, to the tomb :
Weaving to dreams the sexual strife,
And weeping over the web of life.

EPILOGUE.

TO THE ACCUSER, WHO IS THE GOD OF THIS WORLD.

TRULY, my Satan, thou art but a dunce,
    And dost not know the garment from the man ;
Every harlot was a virgin once,
    Nor canst thou ever change Kate into Nan.
Though thou art worshipped by the names divine
    Of Jesus and Jehovah, thou art still
The son of morn in weary night's decline,
    The lost traveller's dream under the hill.

A SONG OF SORROW.

LEAVE, O leave me to my sorrow,
    Here I'll sit and fade away
Till I'm nothing but a spirit,
    And I love this form of clay.
Then if chance along this forest
    Any walk in pathless ways,
Through the gloom he'll see my shadow,
    Hear my voice upon the breeze.

IN A MYRTLE SHADE.

To a lovely myrtle bound,
Blossoms showering all around,
O how weak and weary I
Underneath my myrtle lie !

Why should I be bound to thee,
O my lovely myrtle-tree ?
Love, free love, cannot be bound
To any tree that grows on ground.

FREEDOM AND CAPTIVITY.

Love to faults is always blind,
Always is to joy inclined,
Lawless, wingèd, unconfined,
And breaks all chains from every mind.

The souls of men are bought and sold
In milk-fed infancy for gold,
And youths to slaughter-houses led ;
And beauty, for a bit of bread.

THE TWO THRONES.

I ROSE up at the dawn of day.
" Get thee away ! get thee away !
Pray'st thou for riches ?   Away ! away !
This is the throne of Mammon grey."

I, said " This sure is very odd,
I took it to be the throne of God.
Everything else besides I have,
It's only riches I can crave.

" I have mental joys and mental health,
Mental friends and mental wealth.
I've a wife that I love and that loves me,
I've all but riches bodily.

" I am in God's presence night and day,
He never turns His face away.
The Accuser of Sins by my side does stand,
And he holds my money-bags in his hand.

" For my worldly things God makes him pay,
And he'd pay for more if to him I would pray.
And you may do the worst you can do ;
Be assured, Mr. Devil, I won't pray to you.

" Then if for riches I must not pray,
God knows, I little of prayers need say.
So, as a church is known by its steeple,
If I pray, it must be for other people.

" He says, if I don't worship him for a god,
I shall eat coarser food and go worse shod ;
But as I don't value such things as these,
You must do, Mr. Devil, just as God please."

THE TWO KINDS OF RICHES.

Since all the riches of all this world
   May be gifts from the devil and earthly kings,
I should suspect that I worshipped the devil
   If I thanked God for worldly things.

The countless gold of a merry heart,
   The rubies and pearls of a loving eye,
The idle man never can bring to the mart,
   Nor the cunning hoard up in his treasury.

SMILE AND FROWN.

There is a smile of Love,
   And there is a smile of Deceit,
And there is a smile of smiles
   In which these two smiles meet.

And there is a frown of Hate,
   And there is a frown of Disdain,
And there is a frown of frowns
   Which you strive to forget in vain

For it sticks in the heart's deep core,
   And it sticks in the deep backbone.
And no smile ever was smiled
   But only one smile alone,—

And betwixt the cradle and grave
   It only once smiled can be;
And when it once is smiled,
   There's an end to all misery.

NIGHT AND DAY.

SILENT, silent Night,
Quench the holy light
Of thy torches bright;

For, possessed of Day,
Thousand spirits stray,
That sweet joys betray.

Why should joys be sweet
Used with deceit,
Nor with sorrows meet?

But an honest joy
Doth itself destroy
For a harlot coy.

THE TWO SONGS.

I HEARD an angel singing,
When the day was springing:
" Mercy, pity, and peace,
Are the world's release."

Thus he sang all day
Over the new-mown hay,
Till the sun went down,
And haycocks lookèd brown.

I heard a devil curse
Over the heath and the furze;
" Mercy could be no more
If there were nobody poor,

And pity no more could be
If all were happy as ye :
And mutual fear brings peace.
Misery's increase
Are mercy, pity, peace."

At his curse the sun went down,
And the heavens gave a frown.

THAMES AND OHIO.

WHY should I care for the men of Thames,
And the cheating waters of chartered streams
Or shrink at the little blasts of fear
That the hireling blows into mine ear ?

Though born on the cheating banks of Thames—
Though his waters bathed my infant limbs—
The Ohio shall wash his stains from me ;
I was born a slave, but I go to be free.

THE DEFILED SANCTUARY.

I SAW a chapel all of gold
    That none did dare to enter in,
And many weeping stood without,
    Weeping, mourning, worshipping.

I saw a serpent rise between
    The white pillars of the door,
And he forced and forced and forced
    Till down the golden hinges tore :

And along the pavement sweet,
  Set with pearls and rubies bright,
All his shining length he drew,—
  Till upon the altar white

Vomited his poison out
  On the bread and on the wine.
So I turned into a sty,
  And laid me down among the swine.

SCOFFERS.

Mock on, mock on, Voltaire, Rousseau,
  Mock on, mock on ; 'tis all in vain ;
You throw the dust against the wind,
  And the wind blows it back again.

And every stone becomes a gem
  Reflected in the beams divine ;
Blown back, they blind the mocking eye,
  But still in Israel's paths they shine.

The atoms of Democritus
  And Newton's particles of light
Are sands upon the Red Sea shore,
  Where Israel's tents do shine so bright.

THE GREY MONK.

" I SEE, I see ", the Mother said,
" My children shall die for lack of bread !
What more has the merciless tyrant said ? "
The Monk sat down on her stony bed.

His eye was dry, no tears could flow,
A hollow groan bespoke his woe ;
At length a feeble cry he said :
He trembled and shuddered upon the bed—

" When God commanded this hand to write
In the shadowy hours of deep midnight,
He told me that all I wrote should prove
The bane of all that on earth I love.

" My brother starved between two walls ;
Thy children's cry my soul appals.
I mock at the rack and the grinding chain ;
My bent body mocks at their torturing pain.

" Thy father drew his sword in the North,
With his thousands strong he is marched forth.
Thy brother has armed himself in steel,
To avenge the wrongs thy children feel.

" But vain the sword and vain the bow,
They never can work war's overthrow.
The hermit's prayer and the widow's tear
Alone can free the world from fear."

The hand of vengeance sought the bed
To which the purple tyrant fled ;
The iron hand crushed the tyrant's head,
And became a tyrant in his stead.

Until the tyrant himself relent,
The tyrant who the first black bow bent,
Slaughter shall heap the bloody plain ;
Resistance and war is the tyrant's gain.

But the tear of love and forgiveness sweet,
And submission to death beneath his feet ;
The tear shall melt the sword of steel,
And every wound it has made shall heal.

For the tear is an intellectual thing,
And a sigh is the sword of an Angel King ;
And the bitter groan of a martyr's woe
Is an arrow from the Almighty's bow.

THE EVERLASTING GOSPEL.

THE Vision of Christ that thou dost see,
Is my vision's greatest enemy.
Thine is the Friend of all Mankind,
Mine speaks in Parables to the blind.
Thine loves the same world that mine hates,
Thy heaven-doors are my hell-gates.
Socrates taught what Melitus
Loathed as a nation's bitterest curse.
And Caiaphas was, in his own mind,
A benefactor to mankind.
Doth read the Bible day and night,
But thou readest black where I read white.

**

Was Jesus humble, or did He
Give any proofs of humility ;
Boast of high things with a humble tone,
And give with charity a stone ?

When but a child He ran away,
And left His parents in dismay ;
When they had wandered all day long,
These were the words upon His tongue,
" No earthly parents I confess,
I am doing My Father's business."
When the rich learned Pharisee
Came to consult Him secretly,
Upon his heart with iron pen
He wrote, " Ye must be born again."
He was too proud to take a bribe ;
He spoke with authority, not like a scribe.
He says, with most consummate art,
" Follow Me : I am meek and lowly of heart,"
As that is the only way to escape
The miser's net and the glutton's trap.
He who loves his enemies hates his friends,
This surely was not what Jesus intends,
But the sneaking pride of heroic schools,
And the scribes and Pharisees' virtuous rules ;
But He acts with honest triumphant pride,
And this is the cause that Jesus died.
He did not die with Christian ease,
Asking pardon of His enemies.
If He had, Caiaphas would forgive :
Sneaking submission can always live.
He had only to say that God was the Devil,
And the Devil was God, like a Christian civil.
Mild Christian regrets to the Devil confess
For affronting him thrice in the wilderness.
Like to Priestly and Bacon and Newton,
Poor spiritual knowledge is not worth a button.
He had soon been bloody Cæsar's elf,

And at last He would have been Cæsar himself.
And thus the Gospel St. Isaac confutes,
" God is only known by His attributes.
And as for the indwelling of the Holy Ghost,
Or Christ and His Father, it's all a boast,
Or pride and fallacy of the imagination,
That disdains to follow this world's fashion,"
To teach doubt and experiment,
Certainly was not what Christ meant.

What was He doing all that time
From ten years old to manly prime ?
Was He then idle, or the less
About His father's business ?
Or was His wisdom held in scorn
Before His wrath began to burn
In miracles throughout the land
That quite unnerved the seraph hand ?
If He had been anti-Christ, creeping Jesus,
He'd have done anything to please us :
Gone sneaking into synagogues,
And not used the elders and priests like dogs.
But humble as a lamb or ass
Obeyed Himself to Caiaphas.
God wants not man to humble Himself,
That is the trick of the ancient elf.
This is the race that Jesus ran,
Humble to God, haughty to man ;
Cursing the rulers before the people,
Even to the temple's highest steeple.
And when He humbled Himself to God,
Then descended the cruel rod.
" If thou humblest Thyself thou humblest Me.
Thou also dwellest in eternity.

Thou art a man.   God is no more.
Thine own humanity learn to adore ;
For that is My spirit of life.
Awake, arise to spiritual strife,
And Thy revenge abroad display,
In terrors at the last judgment day.
God's mercy and long-suffering
Are but the sinner to justice to bring.
Thou on the cross for them shall pray,
And take revenge at the last day."
Jesus replied in thunders hurled,
" I never will pray for the world ;
Once I did so when I prayed in the garden,
I wished to take with Me a bodily pardon.
Can that which was of woman born,
In the absence of the morn,
When the soul fell into sleep,
And archangels round did weep,
Shooting out against the light,
Fibres of a deadly night,
Reasoning upon its own dark fiction,
In doubt which is self-contradiction ?
Humility is only doubt,
And does the sun and moon blot out,
Roofing over with thorns and stems
The buried soul and all its gems.
This life's five windows of the soul
Distort the heavens from pole to pole.
And lead you to believe a lie,
When you see *with* not *through* the eye
Which was born in a night to perish in a night,
When the soul slept in beams of light."
John from the wilderness loud cried

Satan gloried in his pride.
" Come", said Satan, " come away,
I'll soon see if You obey.
John for disobedience bled,
But You can turn the stone to bread.
God's high King and God's high Priest
Shall plant their glories in Your breast.
If Caiaphas You will obey,
If Herod You with bloody prey,
Feed with the sacrifice and be
Obedient ; fall down, worship me."
Thunder and lightnings broke around,
And Jesus' voice in the thunder's sound.
" Thus, I seize the spiritual prey,
Ye smiters with disease, give way.
I come your King and God to seize,
Is God a smiter with disease ? "
The God of this World raged in vain,
He bound old Satan in His chain,
And, bursting forth His furious ire,
Became a chariot of fire.
Throughout the land He took His course,
And traced diseases to their source.
He cursed the scribe and Pharisee,
Trampling down hypocrisy ;
Where'er His chariot took its way,
The gates of Death let in the day,
Broke down from every chain a bar,
And Satan in His spiritual war
Dragged at His chariot-wheels.   Loud howl'd
The God of this World.   Louder rolled
The chariot-wheels, and louder still
His voice was heard from Zion's Hill,

And in His hand the scourge shone bright
He scourged the merchant Canaanite
From out the temple of His mind,
And in His body tight did bind
Satan and all his hellish crew ;
And thus with wrath He did subdue,
The serpent bulk of Nature's dross,
Till He had nailed it to the cross.
He took on sin in the virgin's womb,
And put if off on the cross and tomb,
To be worshipped by the Church of Rome.

⁎

Was Jesus chaste, or did He
Give any lessons in chastity ?
The Morning blushed fiery red,
Mary was found in adulterous bed.
Earth groaned beneath, and Heaven above,
Trembled at discovery of love.
Jesus was sitting in Moses' chair.
They brought the trembling woman there.
Moses commands she be stoned to death.
What was the sound of Jesus' breath ?
He laid His hand on Moses' law.
The ancient heavens in silent awe,
Writ with curses from pole to pole.
All away began to roll.
The Earth trembling and naked lay
In secret bed of mortal clay.
On Sinai fell the hand Divine,
Putting back the bloody shrine,
And she heard the breath of God,
As she heard by Eden's flood.
" Good and evil are no more ;

Sinai's trumpets cease to roar.
Cease, finger of God, to write ;
The heavens are not clean in Thy sight.
Thou art good, and Thou alone ;
Nor may the sinner cast one stone.
To be good only, is to be
As God or else a Pharisee.
Thou Angel of the Presence Divine,
That didst create this body of Mine,
Wherefore hast thou writ these laws
And created Hell's dark jaws ?
My presence I will take from thee,
A cold leper thou shalt be,
Though thou wast so pure and bright
That Heaven was not clean in thy sight ;
Though thy oath turned Heaven pale,
Though thy covenant built Hell's jail,
Though thou dost all to chaos roll
With the serpent for its soul.
Still the breath Divine does move,
And the breath Divine is love.
Mary, fear not.   Let Me see
The seven devils that torment thee.
Hide not from My sight thy sin,
That forgiveness thou mayst win.
Has no man condemned thee ? "
" No man, Lord."   " Then what is he
Who shall accuse thee ?   Come ye forth,
Fallen fiends of heavenly birth
That have forgot your ancient love
And driven away My trembling dove.
You shall bow before her feet ;
You shall lick the dust for meet,

And though you cannot love, but hate,
You shall be beggars at love's gate.
What was thy love ?   Let Me see it.
Was it love, or dark deceit ? "
" Love too long from me has fled.
'Twas dark deceit to earn my bread.
'Twas covet, or 'twas custom, or
Some trifle not worth caring for
That they may call a shame and sin
Love's temple that God dwelleth in,
And hide in secret hidden shrine
The naked human form divine,
And render that a lawless thing
On which the soul expands her wing,
But this, O Lord, this was my sin,
When first I let the devils in,
In dark pretence to chastity,
Blaspheming love, blaspheming Thee.
Thence rose secret adulteries,
And thence did covet also rise.
My sin Thou hast forgiven me.
Canst Thou forgive my blasphemy ?
Canst Thou return to this dark hell,
And in my burning bosom dwell ?
And canst Thou die that I may live.
And canst Thou pity and forgive ? "
Then rolled the shadowy man away
From the limbs of Jesus to make them his prey,
An ever-devouring-appetite
Glistering with festering venoms bright,
Saying,—" Crucify this cause of distress,
Who does not keep the secret of holiness !
The mental powers by disease we bind

But He heals the deaf, the dumb, the blind,
Whom God hath afflicted for secret ends.
He comforts and heals and calls them friends."
But when Jesus was crucified,
Then was perfected his galling pride.
In three days he devoured his prey,
And still devours this body of clay.
For dust and clay is the serpent's meat
That never was meant for man to eat.

**
**

Was Jesus born of a vigin pure
With narrow soul and looks demure ?
If He intended to take on sin
His mother should an harlot have been,
Just such a one as Magdalen
With seven devils in her pen.
Or were Jew virgins still more cursed,
And with more suckling devils nursed ?
Or what was it that He took on
That He might bring salvation ?
A body subject to be tempted,
From neither pain nor grief exempted,—
Or such a body as might not feel
The passions that with sinners deal ?
Yes, but they say He never fell.
Ask Caiaphas, for he can tell.
" He mocked the Sabbath, and He mocked
The Sabbath's God, and He unlocked
The evil spirits from their shrines,
And turned fishermen to divines.
O'erturned the tent of secret sins,
And all its golden cords and pins ;
'Tis the bloody shrine of war,

Poured around from star to star,—
Halls of justice, hating vice,
Where the devil combs his lice.
He turned the devils into swine
That He might tempt the Jews to dine ;
Since when a pig has got a look
That for a Jew may be mistook.
' Obey your parents.'   What says He ?
' Woman, what have I to do with thee ?
No earthly parents I confess,
I am doing My father's business.'
He scorned earth's parents, scorned earth's God,
And mocked the one and the other rod ;
His seventy disciples sent
Against religion and government,
They by the sword of Justice fell,
And Him their cruel murderer tell.
He left His father's trade to roam
A wandering vagrant without home,
And thus He others' labours stole
That He might live above control.
The publicans and harlots He
Selected for His company,
And from the adulteress turned away
God's righteous law that lost its prey.''

***

I am sure this Jesus will not do
Either for Englishman or Jew.

TO OLD NOBODADDY.

Why art thou silent and invisible,
    Father of Jealousy ?
Why dost thou hide thyself in clouds
    From every searching eye ?
Why darkness and obscurity
    In all thy words and laws,—
That none dare eat the fruit but from
    The wily serpent's jaws ?
Or is it because secrecy
    Gains feminine applause ?

BARREN BLOSSOM.

I feared the fury of my wind
    Would blight all blossoms fair and true,
And my sun it shined and shined,
    And my wind it never blew.

But a blossom fair or true
    Was not found on any tree ;
For all blossoms grew and grew
    Fruitless, false, though fair to see.

OPPORTUNITY.

He who bends to himself a joy
Does the winged life destroy ;
But he who kisses the joy as it flies
Lives in eternity's sunrise.

If you trap the moment before it's ripe,
The tears of repentance you'll certainly wipe ;
But, if once you let the ripe moment go,
You can never wipe off the tears of woe.

LOVE'S SECRET.

NEVER seek to tell thy love,
  Love that never told shall be ;
For the gentle wind does move
  Silently, invisibly.

I told my love, I told my love,
  I told her all my heart,
Trembling, cold, in ghastly fears.
  Ah ! she did depart !

Soon after she has gone from me,
  A traveller came by,
Silently, invisibly :
  He took her with a sigh.

THE WILL AND THE WAY.

I ASKED a thief to steal me a peach :
  He turned up his eyes.
I asked a lithe lady to lie her down :
  Holy and meek, she cries.

As soon as I went,
  An Angel came,
He winked at the thief,
  And smiled at the dame :

And, without one word spoke.
  Had a peach from the tree,
And 'twixt earnest and joke
  Enjoyed the lady.

CUPID.

WHY was Cupid a boy,
  And why a boy was he ?
He snould have been a girl,
  For aught that I can see.

For he shoots with his bow,
  And a girl shoots with her eye ;
And they both are merry and glad
  And laugh when we do cry.

And to make Cupid a boy
  Was surely a woman's plan,
For a boy never learns to mock
  Till he has become a man :

And then he is so pierced through
  And wounded with arrowy smarts,
That the whole business of his life,
  Is to pick out the heads of the darts.

THE THISTLES AND THORNS.

I LAID me down upon a bank,
  Where love lay sleeping ;
I heard among the rushes dank,
  Weeping, weeping.

Then I went to the heath and the wild,
  To the thistles and thorns of the waste ;
And they told me how they were beguiled,
  Driven out, and compelled to be chaste.

THE GOLDEN NET.

BENEATH the white-thorn's lovely may,
Three virgins at the break of day.—
" Whither, young man, whither away ?
Alas for woe ! alas for woe ! "
They cry, and tears for ever flow.
The one was clothed in flames of fire,
The other clothed in iron wire ;
The other clothed in tears and sighs.
Dazzling bright before my eyes.
They bore a net of golden twine
To hang upon the branches fine.
Pitying, I wept to see the woe
That love and beauty undergo—
To be consumed in flames of fire
And in unsatisfied desire,
And in tears clothed night and day
It melted all my soul away.
When they saw my tears, a smile
That did heaven itself beguile
Bore the golden net aloft,
As by downy pinions soft,
Over the morning of my day.
Underneath the net I stray,
Now entreating Flaming-fire,
Now entreating Iron wire,
Now entreating Tears and Sighs.—
O, when will the morning rise ?

THE CRYSTAL CABINET.

THE maiden caught me in the wild,
    Where I was dancing merrily ;
She put me into her cabinet,
    And locked me up with a golden key.

This cabinet is formed of gold,
    And pearl and crystal shining bright,
And within it opens into a world
    And a little lovely moony night.

Another England there I saw,
    Another London with its Tower,
Another Thames and other hills,
    And another pleasant Surrey bower.

Another maiden like herself,
    Translucent, lovely, shining clear,
Threefold, each in the other closed—
    O, what a pleasant trembling fear !

O, what a smile !   A threefold smile
    Filled me that like a flame I burned ;
I bent to kiss the lovely maid,
    And found a threefold kiss returned.

I strove to seize the inmost form
    With ardour fierce and hands of flame,
But burst the crystal cabinet,
    And like a weeping babe became :

A weeping babe upon the wild,
    And weeping woman pale reclined,
And in the outward air again.
    I filled with woes the passing wind.

THE MENTAL TRAVELLER.

I TRAVELLED through a land of men
   A land of men and women too ;
And heard and saw such dreadful things
   As cold earth wanderers never knew.

For there the babe is born in joy
   That was begotten in dire woe ;
Just as we reap in joy the fruit
   Which we in bitter tears did sow.

And, if the babe is born a boy,
   He's given to a woman old,
Who nails him down upon a rock,
   Catches his shrieks in cups of gold.

She binds iron thorns around his head,
   She pierces both his hands and feet,
She cuts his heart out at his side,
   To make it feel both cold and heat.

Her fingers number every nerve,
   Just as a miser counts his gold ;
She lives upon his shrieks and cries,
   And she grows young as he grows old.

Till he becomes a bleeding youth,
   And she becomes a virgin bright ;
Then he rends up his manacles,
   And binds her down for his delight.

He plants himself in all her nerves,
   Just as a husbandman his mould,
And she becomes his dwelling-place
   And garden fruitful seventy-fold.

An aged shadow soon he fades,
   Wandering round an earthly cot,
Full-fillèd all with gems and gold
   Which he by industry had got.

And these are the gems of the human soul,
   The rubies and pearls of a lovesick eye,
The countless gold of the aching heart,
   The martyr's groan and the lover's sigh.

They are his meat, they are his drink ;
   He feeds the beggar and the poor ;
To the wayfaring traveller
   For ever open is his door.

His grief is their eternal joy,
   They make the roofs and walls to ring ;
Till from the fire upon the hearth
   A little female babe doth spring.

And she is all of solid fire
   And gems and gold, that none his hand
Dares stretch to touch her baby form,
   Or wrap her in his swaddling-band.

But she comes to the man she loves,
   If young or old or rich or poor ;
They soon drive out the aged host,
   A beggar at another's door.

He wanders weeping far away,
   Until some other take him in ;
Oft blind and age-bent, sore distressed,
   Until he can a maiden win.

And, to allay his freezing age,
  The poor man takes her in his arms ;
The cottage fades before his sight,
  The garden and its lovely charms.

The guests are scattered through the land ;
  For the eye altering alters all ;
The senses roll themselves in fear,
  And the flat earth becomes a ball.

The stars, sun, moon, all shrink away ;
  A desert vast without a bound,
And nothing left to eat or drink,
  And a dark desert all around ;

The honey of her infant lips,
  The bread and wine of her sweet smile,
The wild game of her roving eye,
  Do him to infancy beguile.

For as he eats and drinks, he grows
  Younger and younger every day,
And on the desert wild they both
  Wander in terror and dismay.

Like the wild stag she flies away ;
  Her fear plants many a thicket wild,
While he pursues her night and day
  By various art of love beguiled ;

By various arts of love and hate,
  Till the wild desert planted o'er
With labyrinths of wayward love,
  Where roam the lion, wolf and boar

Till he becomes a wayward babe,
　　And she a weeping woman old ;
Then many a lover wanders here,
　　The sun and stars are nearer rolled ;

The trees bring forth sweet ecstasy
　　To all who in the desert roam ;
Till many a city there is built,
　　And many a pleasant shepherd's home.

But, when they find the frowning babe,
　　Terror strikes through the region wide ;
They cry—" The babe—the babe is born !
　　And flee away on every side.

For who dare touch the frowning form,
　　His arm is withered to its root ;
Bears, lions, wolves, all howling flee,
　　And every tree doth shed its fruit.

And none can touch that frowning form
　　Except it be a woman old ;
She nails him down upon the rock,
　　And all is done as I have told.

SPECTRE AND EMANATION.

1.

My Spectre before me night and day
Like a wild beast guards my way.
My Emanation far within
Weeps incessantly for my sin.

2.

A fathomless and boundless deep ;
There we wonder, there we weep.
On the hungry craving wind
My Spectre follows thee behind.

3.

He scents thy footsteps in the snow,
Wheresoever thou dost go,
Through the wintry hail and rain.
When wilt thou return again ?

4.

Dost thou not in pride and scorn
Fill with tempests all my morn,
And with jealousies and fears,
Fill my pleasant nights with tears ?

5.

Seven of my sweet loves thy knife
Has bereaved of their life.
Their marble tombs I build with fears,
And with cold and shadowy tears.

6.

Seven more loves weep night and day
Round the tombs where my loves lay,
And seven more loves attend at night
Around my couch with torches bright.

7.

And seven more loves in my bed
Crown with vine my mournful head,
Pitying and forgiving all
My transgressions, great and small.

8.

When wilt thou return and view
My loves, and them to life renew?
When wilt thou return and live?
When wilt thou pity as I forgive?

9.

"Never, never I return.
Still for victory I burn.
Living, thee alone I'll have,
And when dead I'll be thy grave.

10.

"Through the Heaven and Earth and Hell—
Thou shalt never, never never quell,—
I will fly and thou pursue,
Night and morn the flight renew."

11.

Till I turn from female love
And root up the infernal grove
I shall never worthy be
To step into Eternity.

12.

And I to end thy cruel mocks
Annihilate thee on the rocks,
And another form create
To be subservient to my fate.

13.

Let us agree to give up love
And root up the infernal grove,
Then shall we return and see
The worlds of happy Eternity.

14.

And throughout all Eternity
I forgive you, you forgive me.
As our dear Redeemer said :
This the wine and this the bread.

WILLIAM BOND

I WONDER whether the girls are mad,
  And I wonder whether they mean to kill,
And I wonder if William Bond will die,
  For assuredly he is very ill.

He went to church on a May morning,
  Attended by fairies one, two, and three,
But the angels of Providence drove them away,
  And he returned home in misery.

He went not out to the field nor fold,
  He went not out to the village nor town,
But he came home in a black, black cloud,
  And took to his bed, and there lay down.

And an angel of Providence at his feet,
    And an angel of Providence at his head,
And in the midst a black, black cloud,
    And in the midst the sick man on his bed.

And on his right hand was Mary Green,
    And on his left hand was his sister Jane,
And their tears fell through the black, black cloud
    To drive away the sick man's pain,

" O, William, if thou dost another love,
    Dost another love better than poor Mary,
Go and take that other to be thy wife,
    And Mary Green shall her servant be."

" Yes, Mary, I do another love,
    Another I love far better than thee,
And another I will have for my wife :
    Then what have I to do with thee ?

" For thou art melancholy pale,
    And on thy head is the cold moon's shine,
But she is ruddy and bright as day,
    And the sunbeams dazzle from her eyne."

Mary trembled, and Mary chilled,
    And Mary fell down on the right-hand floor,
That William Bond and his sister Jane
    Scarce could recover Mary more.

When Mary woke and found her laid
    On the right hand of her William dear,
On the right hand of his loved bed,
    And saw her William Bond so near ;

The fairies that fled from William Bond
   Danced around her shining head ;
They danced over the pillow white,
   And the angels of Providence left the bed.

" I thought Love lived in the hot sunshine,
   But O he lives in the moony light !
I thought to find Love in the heat of day,
   But sweet Love is the comforter of night.

" Seek Love in the pity of others' woe,
   In the gentle relief of another's care,
In the darkness of night and the winter's snow,
   With the naked and outcast,—seek Love there."

MARY,

SWEET Mary, the first time she ever was there,
Came into the ball-room among the fair ;
The young men and maidens around her throng,
And these are the words upon every tongue :

" An angel is here from the heavenly climes,
Or again return the golden times ;
Her eyes out shine every brilliant ray,
She opens her lips—" 'tis the month of May."

Mary moves in soft beauty and conscious delight,
To augment with sweet smiles all the joys of the night,
Nor once blushes to own to the rest of the fair
That sweet love and beauty are worthy our care.

In the morning the villagers rose with delight,
And repeated with pleasure the joys of the night,
And Mary arose among friends to be free,
But no friend from henceforward thou, Mary, shalt see.

Some said she was proud, some called her a whore,
And some when she passed by shut-to the door ;
A damp cold came o'er her, her blushes all fled,
Her lilies and roses are blighted and shed.

" O, why was I born with a different face ?
Why was I not born like this envious race ?
Why did Heaven adorn me with bountiful hand,
And then set me down in an envious land ?

" To be weak as a lamb and smooth as a dove,
And not to raise envy, is called Christian love ;
But, if you raise envy, your merit's to blame
For planting such spite in the weak and the tame.

" I will humble my beauty, I will not dress fine,
I will keep from the ball, and my eyes shall not shine ;
And, if any girl's lover forsake her for me,
I'll refuse him my hand, and from envy be free."

She went out in the morning attired plain and neat ;
" Proud Mary's gone mad ", said the child in the
      street ;
She went out in the morning in plain neat attire,
And came home in the evening bespattered with mire.

She trembled and wept, sitting on the bedside,
She forgot it was night, and she trembled and cried ;
She forgot it was night, she forgot it was morn,
Her soft memory imprinted with faces of scorn ;

With faces of scorn and with eyes of disdain,
Like foul fiends inhabiting Mary's mild brain ;
She remembers no face like the human divine ;
All faces have envy, sweet Mary, but thine.

And thine is a face of sweet love in despair,
And thine is a face of mild sorrow and care,
And thine is a face of wild terror and fear
That shall never be quiet till laid on its bier.

OLD ENGLISH HOSPITALITY.

THIS City and this country have brought forth many
    Mayors
To sit in state and give forth laws out of their old oak
    chairs,
With face as brown as any nut with drinking of strong
    ale—
Old English hospitality, O then it did not fail.

With scarlet gowns and broad gold lace, would make
    a yeoman sweat ;
With stockings rolled above their knees, and shoes as
    black as jet ;
With eating beef and drinking beer, O they were stout
    and hale—
Old English hospitality, O then it did not fail.

Thus sitting at the table wide the Mayor and Aldermen
Were fit to give laws to the city : each eat as much as
    ten.
The hungry poor entered the hall to eat good beef and
    ale—
Good English hospitality, O then it did not fail.

LOS THE TERRIBLE.

With happiness stretched across the hills
In a cloud that dewy sweetness distils,
With a blue sky spread over with wings,
And a mild sun that mounts and sings ;
With trees and fields full of fairy elves,
And little devils who fight for themselves,
Remembering the verses that Hayley sung
When my heart knocked against the root of my tongue.
With angels planted in hawthorn bowers,
And God himself in the passing Hours ;
With silver angels across my way,
And golden demons that none can stay ;
With my father hovering upon the wind,
And my brother Robert just behind,
And my brother John, the evil one,
In a black cloud making his moan ;
(Though dead, they appear upon my path.
Notwithstanding my terrible wrath ;
They beg, they entreat, they drop their tears,
Filled full of hopes, filled full of fears ;)
With a thousand angels upon the wind,
Pouring disconsolate from behind
To drive them off,—and before my way
A frowning Thistle implores my stay.
What to others a trifle appears,
Fills me full of smiles or tears ;
For double the vision my eyes do see,
And a double vision is always with me.
With my inward eye, 'tis an old man grey ;
With my outward, a thistle across my way.

" If thou goest back, " the Thistle said,
" Thou art to endless woe betrayed ;
For here does Theotormon lour,
And here is Enitharmon's bower,
And Los the terrible thus hath sworn,
Because thou backward dost return,
Poverty, envy, old age, and fear,
Shall bring thy wife upon a bier ;
And Butts shall give what Fuseli gave,
A dark black rock and a gloomy cave."
I struck the thistle with my foot,
And broke him up from his delving root.
" Must the duties of life each other cross ?
Must every joy be dung and dross ?
Must my dear Butts feel cold neglect
Because I give Hayley his due respect ?
Must Flaxman look upon me as wild,
And all my friends be with doubts beguiled ;
Must my wife live in my sister's bane,
Or my sister survive on my Love's pain ?
The curses of Los, the terrible shade,
And his dismal terrors, make me afraid."

So I spoke, and struck in my wrath
The old man weltering upon my path.
Then Los appeared in all his power :
In the sun he appeared, descending before
My face in fierce flames ; in my double sight,
'Twas outward a sun,—inward, Los in his might.
" My hands are laboured day and night,
And ease comes never in my sight.
My wife has no indulgence given,
Except what comes to her from heaven.

We eat little, we drink less ;
This earth breeds not our happiness.
Another sun feeds our life's streams ;
We are not warmèd with thy beams.
Thou measurest not the time to me,
Nor yet the space that I do see :
My mind is not with thy light arrayed ;
Thy terrors shall not make me afraid."

When I had my defiance given,
The sun stood trembling in heaven ;
The moon, that glowed remote below,
Became leprous and white as snow ;
And every soul of man on the earth
Felt affliction and sorrow and sickness and dearth.
Los flamed in my path, and the sun was hot
With the bows of my mind and the arrows of thought :
My bowstring fierce with ardour breathes,
My arrows glow in their golden sheaves.
My brother and father march before ;
The heavens drop with human gore.
Now I a fourfold vision see,
And a fourfold vision is given to me.
'Tis fourfold in my supreme delight,
And threefold in solt Beulah's night,
And twofold always.   May God us keep
From single vision, and Newton's sleep !

DEDICATION OF THE DESIGNS TO BLAIR'S "GRAVE."

To Queen Charlotte.

The door of Death is made of gold,
That mortal eyes cannot behold :
But, when the mortal eyes are closed,
And cold and pale the limbs reposed,
The soul awakes, and, wondering, sees
In her mild hand the golden keys.
The grave is heaven's golden gate,
And rich and poor around it wait :
O Shepherdess of England's fold,
Behold this gate of pearl and gold !

To dedicate to England's Queen
The visions that my soul has seen,
And by her kind permission bring
What I have borne on solemn wing
From the vast regions of the grave.
Before her throne my wings I wave,
Bowing before my sovereign's feet.
The Grave produced these blossoms sweet,
In mild repose from earthly strife ;
The blossoms of eternal life.

FOR A PICTURE OF THE LAST JUDGMENT.

DEDICATION.

The caverns of the Grave I've seen,
And these I showed to England's Queen,
But now the caves of Hell I view,—
Whom shall I dare to show them to ?
What mighty soul in beauty's form
Shall dauntless view the infernal storm ?
Egremont's Countess can control
The flames of hell that round me roll.
If she refuse, I still go on,
Till the heavens and earth are gone ;
Still admired by noble minds,
Followed by Envy on the winds.
Re-engraved time after time,
Ever in their youthful prime,
My designs unchanged remain ;
Time may rage, but rage in vain ;
For above Time's troubled fountains,
On the great Atlantic mountains,
In my golden house on high,
There they hide eternally.

COUPLETS AND FRAGMENTS.

1.

I WALKED abroad on a snowy day,
I wooed the soft snow with me to play,
She played and she melted in all her prime ;
And the winter called it a dreadful crime.

2.

What is it men in women do require ?
The lineaments of gratified desire.
What is it women do in men require ?
The lineaments of gratified desire.

3.

Abstinence sows sand all over
The ruddy limbs and flaming hair ;
But desire gratified
Plants fruits of life and beauty there.

4.

The look of love alarms,
Because 'tis filled with fire ;
But the look of soft deceit
Shall win the lover's hire :
Soft deceit and idleness,
These are beauty's sweetest dress.

5.

To Chloe's breast young Cupid slily stole,
But he crept in at Myra's pocket-hole.

6.

Fortune favours the brave, old proverbs say ;
But not with money, that is not the way.
Turn back, turn back, you travel all in vain ;
Turn through the Iron Gate down Sneaking Lane.

7.

The Sword sang on the barren heath,
   The Sickle in the fruitful field :
The Sword he sang a song of death,
   But could not make the Sickle yield.

8.

Great things are done when men and mountains meet ;
These are not done by jostling in the street.

9.

The errors of a wise man make your rule,
Rather than the perfections of a fool.

10.

Some people admire the work of a fool,
For it's sure to keep your judgment cool :
It does not reproach you with want of wit ;
It is not like a lawyer serving a writ.

11.

He's a blockhead who wants a proof of what he can't
   perceive,
And he's a fool who tries to make such a blockhead
   believe.

12.

If e'er I grow to man's estate,
O give to me a woman's fate !
May I govern all, both great and small,
Have the last word, and take the wall !

13.

Let us approach the sighing dawns,
  With many pleasing wiles—
If a woman does not fear your frowns,
  She will not reward your smiles.

14.

Her whole life is an epigram—smack, smooth, and
  nobly penned,
Plaited quite neat to catch applause, with a strong
  noose at the end.

15.

The Angel that presided at my birth
Said : " Little creature, formed of joy and mirth,
Go, love without the help of any thing on earth."

16.

At a friend's errors anger show,
Mirth at the errors of a foe.
Anger and wrath my bosom rends :
I thought them the errors of friends.
But all my limbs with warmth glow,
I find them the errors of the foe.

17.

You say reserve and modesty he has,
Whose heart is iron, his head wood, and his face brass-
The fox, the owl, the beetle, and the bat
By sweet reserve and modesty get fat.

18.

Here lies John Trot, the friend of all mankind ;
He has not left one enemy behind.
Friends *were* quite hard to find, old authors say ;
But now they stand in everybody's way.

19.

Stothard in childhood on the nursery floor
Was extreme old and most extremely poor ;
He has grown great and rich, and what he will,
He is extreme old and is extreme poor still.

20.

Of Hayley's birth this was the happy lot :
His mother on his father him begot.

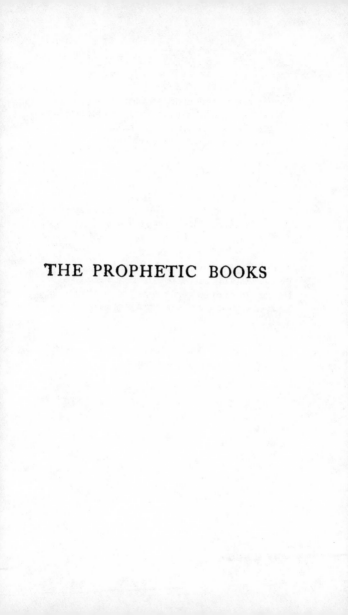

THE PROPHETIC BOOKS

THE PROPHETIC BOOKS

TIRIEL

I.

AND aged Tiriel stood before the gates of his beautiful
    palace,
With Myratana, once the Queen of all the western
    plains ;
But now his eyes were darkened, and his wife fading
    in death.
They stood before their once delightful palace ; and
    thus the voice
Of aged Tiriel arose, that his sons might hear in their
    gates.

" Accursed race of Tiriel ! behold your father ;
Come forth and look on her that bore you. Come,
    you accursed sons.
In my weak arms I here have borne your dying mother ;
Come forth, sons of the curse, come forth ! see the
    death of Myratana."

His sons ran from their gates, and saw their aged
    parents stand ;
And thus the eldest son of Tiriel raised his mighty
    voice :—

" Old man ! unworthy to be called the father of Tiriel's
    race !

For every one of those thy wrinkles, each of those
    grey hairs,

Are cruel as death, and as obdurate as the devouring
    pit !

Why should thy sons care for thy curses, thou accursed
    man ?

Were we not slaves till we rebelled ? Who cares
    for Tiriel's curse ?

His blessing was a cruel curse ; his curse may be a
    blessing."

He ceased. The aged man raised up his right hand
    to the heavens :

His left supported Myratana, shrinking in pangs of
    death.

The orbs of his large eyes he opened, and thus his
    voice went forth :—

" Serpents, not sons, wreathing around the bones of
    Tiriel !

Ye worms of death, feasting upon your aged parent's
    flesh,

Listen, and hear your mother's groans. No more
    accursed sons

She bears ; she groans not at the birth of Heuxos or
    Yuva.

These are the groans of death, ye serpents ! these are
    the groans of death !

Nourished with milk, ye serpents, nourished with
    mother's tears and cares !

Look at my eyes, blind as the orbless skull among the
    stones ;

Look at my bald head. Hark, listen, ye serpents,
listen ! . . .

What, Myratana ! What, my wife ! O soul ! O
spirit ! O fire !

What, Myratana, art thou dead ? Look here, ye
serpents, look !

The serpents sprung from her own bowels have drained
her dry as this.

Curse on your ruthless heads, for I will bury her even
here ! "

So saying, he began to dig a grave with his aged hands :
But Heuxos called a son of Zazel to dig their mother
a grave.

" Old cruelty, desist, and let us dig a grave for thee.

Thou hast refused our charity, thou hast refused our
food,

Thou hast refused our clothes, our beds, our houses
for thy dwelling,

Choosing to wander like a son of Zazel in the rocks.

Why dost thou curse ? Is not the curse now come
upon thine head ?

Was it not thou enslaved the sons of Zazel ? and they
have cursed,

And now thou feel'st it ! Dig a grave, and let us
bury our mother."

" There, take the body, cursed sons ! and may the
heavens rain wrath,

As thick as northern fogs, around your gates, to choke
you up !

That you may lie as now your mother lies—like dogs,
cast out.

The stink of your dead carcases annoying man and beast,

Till your white bones are bleached with age for a memorial.

No! your remembrance shall perish; for, when your carcases

Lie stinking on the earth, the buriers shall arise from the East,

And not a bone of all the sons of Tiriel remain.

Bury your mother, but you cannot bury the curse of Tiriel."

He ceased, and darkling o'er the mountains sought his pathless way.

2.

He wandered day and night. To him both day and night were dark:

The sun he felt, but the bright moon was now a useless globe.

O'er mountains and through vales of woe the blind and aged man

Wandered, till he that leadeth all led him to the vales of Har.

And Har and Heva, like two children, sat beneath the oak.

Mnetha, now aged, waited on them, and brought them food and clothing.

But they were as the shadow of Har, and as the years forgotten;

Playing with flowers and running after birds they spent the day,

And in the night like infants slept, delighted with infant dreams.

Soon as the blind wanderer entered the pleasant gar-
dens of Har,

They ran weeping, like frighted infants, for refuge in
Mnetha's arms.

The blind man felt his way, and cried: "Peace to
these open doors!

Let no one fear, for poor blind Tiriel hurts none but
himself.

Tell me, O friends, where am I now, and
in what pleasant place?"

"This is the valley of Har", said Mnetha, "and this
the tent of Har.

Who art thou, poor blind man, that takest the name
of Tiriel on thee?

Tiriel is King of all the West. Who art thou? I
am Mnetha;

And this is Har and Heva, trembling like infants
by my side."

"I know Tiriel is King of the West, and there he
lives in joy.

No matter who I am, O Mnetha! If thou hast any
food,

Give it me, for I cannot stay,—my journey is far from
hence."

Then Har said: "O my mother Mnetha, venture
not so near him,

For he is the king of rotten wood, and of the bones
of death;

He wanders without eyes, and passes through thick
walls and doors.

Thou shalt not smite my mother Mnetha, O thou eye-
less man."

" A wanderer, I beg for food.   You see I cannot weep.
I cast away my staff, the kind companion of my travel,
And I kneel down that you may see I am a harmless
    man."

He kneeled down. And Mnetha said : " Come,
    Har and Heva, rise :
He is an innocent old man, and hungry with his travel."

Then Har arose, and laid his hand upon old Tiriel's
    head.

" God bless thy poor bald pate, God bless thy hollow
    winking eyes,
God bless thy shrivelled beard, God bless thy many-
    wrinkled forehead !
Thou hast no teeth, old man ! and thus I kiss thy
    sleek bald head.
Heva, come kiss his bald head, for he will not hurt
    us, Heva."

Then Heva came, and took old Tiriel in her mother's
    arms.

" Bless thy poor eyes, old man, and bless the old
    father of Tiriel !
Thou art my Tiriel's old father ; I know thee through
    thy wrinkles,
Because thou smellest like the fig-tree, thou smellest
    like ripe figs.
How didst thou lose thy eyes, old Tiriel ? Bless
    thy wrinkled face ! "

Mnetha said : " Come in, aged wanderer ; tell us
    of thy name.
Why shouldst thou conceal thyself from those of
    thine own flesh ? "

" I am not of this region ", said Tiriel dissemblingly.

" I am an aged wanderer, once father of a race
Far in the North ; but they were wicked, and were
all destroyed,
And I their father sent an outcast. I have told you
all :
Ask me no more, I pray, for grief hath sealed my
precious sight."

" O Lord ! " said Mnetha, " how I tremble ! Are
there then more people,
More human creatures on this earth, beside the sons
of Har ? "

" No more ", said Tiriel, " but I, remain on all this
globe ;
And I remain an outcast. Hast thou anything to
drink ? "
Then Mnetha gave him milk and fruits, and they sat
down together.

3

They sat and ate, and Har and Heva smiled on Tiriel.

" Thou art a very old old man, but I am older than
thou.
How came thine hair to leave thy forehead, how came
thy face so brown ?
My hair is very long, my beard doth cover all my
breast.
God bless thy piteous face ! To count the wrinkles
in thy face
Would puzzle Mnetha. Bless thy face, for thou art
Tiriel ! "

" Tiriel I never saw but once. I sat with him and
    ate ;

He was as cheerful as a prince, and gave me enter-
    tainment.

But long I stayed not at his palace, for I am forced
    to wander."

" What ! wilt thou leave us too ? " said Heva. " Thou
    shalt not leave us too,

For we have many sports to show thee, and many
    songs to sing ;

And after dinner we will walk into the cage of Har,

And thou shalt help us to catch birds, and gather
    them ripe cherries ;

Then let thy name be Tiriel, and never leave us more."

" If thou dost go ", said Har, " I wish thine eyes may
    see thy folly.

My sons have left me.—Did thine leave thee ? O
    'twas very cruel ! "

" No, venerable man ", said Tiriel, " ask me not such
    things,

For thou dost make my heart to bleed. My sons
    were not like thine,

But worse. O never ask me more, or I must flee
    away."

" Thou shalt not go ", said Heva, " till thou hast seen
    our singing-birds,

And heard Har sing in the great cage, and slept upon
    our fleeces.

Go not, for thou art so like Tiriel that I love thine
    head,

Though it is wrinkled like the earth parched with
    the summer heat."

Then Tiriel rose up from the seat, and said : " God
    bless these tents !
My journey is o'er rocks and mountains, not in pleasant
    vales ;
I must not sleep nor rest, because of madness and
    dismay."

And Mnetha said : " Thou must not go to wander
    dark alone,
But dwell with us, and let us be to thee instead of
    eyes,
And I will bring thee food, old man, till death shall
    call thee hence."

Then Tiriel frowned, and answered : " Did I not
    command you saying,
Madness and deep dismay possess the heart of the
    blind man,
The wanderer who seeks the woods, leaning upon
    his staff ? "

Then Mnetha, trembling at his frowns, led him to
    the tent-door,
And gave to him his staff, and blessed him. He went
    on his way.

But Har and Heva stood and watched him till he
    entered the wood ;
And then they went and wept to Mnetha, but they
    soon forgot their tears.

4.

Over the weary hills the blind man took his lonely
    way ;
To him the day and night alike was dark and desolate.
But far he had not gone when Ijim from his woods
    came down,
Met him at entrance of the forest, in a dark and lonely
    way.

" Who art thou, eyeless wretch, that thus obstructest
    the lion's path ?
Ijim shall rend thy feeble joints, thou tempter of
    dark Ijim !
Thou hast the form of Tiriel, but I know thee well
    enough !
Stand from my path, foul fiend !   Is this the last of
    thy deceits—
To be a hypocrite, and stand in shape of a blind beg-
    gar ? "

The blind man heard his brother's voice, and kneeled
    down on his knee.

" O brother Ijim, if it is thy voice that speaks to me,—
Smite not thy brother Tiriel, though weary of his life.
My sons have smitten me already ; and, if thou smitest
    me,
The curse that rolls over their heads will rest itself
    on thine.
'Tis now seven years since in my palace I beheld thy
    face."

" Come, thou dark fiend, I dare thy cunning ! know
    that Ijim scorns
To smite thee in the form of helpless age and eyeless
    policy ;

Rise up, for I discern thee, and I dare thy eloquent
   tongue.

Come, I will lead thee on thy way, and use thee as a
   scoff."

" O brother Ijim, thou beholdest wretched Tiriel :

Kiss me, my brother, and then leave me to wander
   desolate ! "

" No, artful fiend, but I will lead thee ; dost thou
   want to go ?

Reply not, lest I bind thee with the green flags of the
   brook ;

Ay, now thou art discovered, I will use thee like a
   slave."

When Tiriel heard the words of Ijim, he sought not
   to reply :

He knew 'twas vain, for Ijim's words were as the
   voice of Fate.

And they went on together, over hills, through woody
   dales,

Blind to the pleasures of the sight, and deaf to warbling
   birds.

All day they walked, and all the night beneath the
   pleasant moon,

Westwardly journeying, till Tiriel grew weary with
   his travel.

" O Ijim, I am faint and weary, for my knees forbid

To bear me further.   Urge me not, lest I should die
   with travel.

A little rest I crave, a little water from a brook,

Or I shall soon discover that I am a mortal man,

And thou wilt lose thy once-loved Tiriel.   Alas !
   how faint I am ! "

" Impudent fiend ! " said Ijim, " hold thy glib and
　　eloquent tongue ;—
Tiriel is a king, and thou the tempter of dark Ijim.
Drink of this running brook, and I will bear thee on
　　my shoulders."

He drank ; and Ijim raised him up, and bore him on
　　his shoulders.
All day he bore him ; and, when evening drew her
　　solemn curtain,
Entered the gates of Tiriel's palace, and stood and
　　called aloud.

" Heuxos, come forth ! I here have brought the
　　fiend that troubles Ijim.
Look ! know'st thou aught of this grey beard, or of
　　these blinded eyes ? "

Heuxos and Lotho ran forth at the sound of Ijim's
　　voice,
And saw their aged father borne upon his mighty
　　shoulders.
Their eloquent tongues were dumb, and sweat stood
　　on their trembling limbs ;
They knew 'twas vain to strive with Ijim. They
　　bowed and silent stood.

" What, Heuxos ! call thy father, for I mean to sport
　　to-night.
This is the hypocrite that sometimes roars a dreadful
　　lion ;
Then I have rent his limbs, and left him rotting in
　　the forest
For birds to eat. But I have scarce departed from
　　the place

But like a tiger he would come, and so I rent him too.

Then like a river he would seek to drown me in his waves,

But soon I buffeted the torrent ; anon like to a cloud

Fraught with the swords of lightning, but I braved the vengeance too.

Then he would creep like a bright serpent, till around my neck

While I was sleeping he would twine : I squeezed his poisonous soul.

Then like a toad or like a newt would whisper in my ears ;

Or like a rock stood in my way, or like a poisonous shrub.

At last I caught him in the form of Tiriel blind and old,

And so I'll keep him. Fetch your father, fetch forth Myratana."

They stood confounded, and thus Tiriel raised his silver voice.

" Serpents, not sons, why do you stand ? Fetch hither Tiriel,

Fetch hither Myratana, and delight yourselves with scoffs ;

For poor blind Tiriel is returned, and this much-injured head

Is ready for your bitter taunts. Come forth, sons of the curse ! "

Meantime the other sons of Tiriel ran around their father,

Confounded at the terrible strength of Ijim. They knew 'twas vain,

Both spear and shield were useless, and the coat of
    iron mail,
When Ijim stretched his mighty arm ; the arrow
    from his limbs
Rebounded, and the piercing sword broke on his
    naked flesh.

" Then it is true, Heuxos, that thou hast turned thy
    aged parent
To be the sport of wintry winds ", said Ijim : " is
    this true ?
It is a lie, and I am like the tree torn by the wind,
Thou eyeless fiend and you dissemblers ! Is this
    Tiriel's house ?
It is as false as Matha, and as dark as vacant Orcus.
Escape, ye fiends, for Ijim will not lift his hand against
    ye."

So saying, Ijim gloomy turned his back, and silent
    sought
The secret forests, and all night wandered in desolate
    ways.

5.

And aged Tiriel stood and said : " Where does the
    thunder sleep ?
Where doth he hide his terrible head ? and his swift
    and fiery daughters,
Where do they shroud their fiery wings, and the
    terrors of their hair ?
Earth, thus I stamp thy bosom ! rouse the earthquake
    from his den,
To raise his dark and burning visage through the
    cleaving ground,

To thrust these towers with his shoulders ! Let his
    fiery dogs
Rise from the centre, belching flames and roaring
    dark smoke !
Where art thou, Pestilence, that bathest in fogs and
    standing lakes ?
Raise up thy sluggish limbs, and let the loathsomest
    of poisons
Drop from thy garments as thou walkest, wrapped
    in yellow clouds !
Here take thy seat in this wide court ; let it be strewn
    with dead ;
And sit and smile upon these cursed sons of Tiriel !
Thunder, and fire, and pestilence, hear you not Tiriel's
    curse ? "

He ceased. The heavy clouds confused rolled round
    the lofty towers,
Discharging their enormous voices at the father's
    curse.
The earth trembled, fires belched from the yawning
    clefts,
And, when the shaking ceased, a fog possessed the
    accursed clime.

The cry was great in Tiriel's palace. His five daughters
    ran,
And caught him by the garments, weeping with cries
    of bitter woe.

" Ay, now you feel the curse, you cry ! but may all
    ears be deaf
As Tiriel's, and all eyes as blind as Tiriel's, to your
    woes !

May never stars shine on your roofs, may never sun
    nor moon
Visit you, but eternal fogs hover around your walls !—
Hela, my youngest daughter, thou shalt lead me from
    this place ;
And let the curse fall on the rest, and wrap them up
    together ! "

He ceased, and Hela led her father from the noisome
    place.
In haste they fled, while all the sons and daughters
    of Tiriel,
Chained in thick darkness, uttered cries of mourning
    all the night.
And in the morning, lo ! an hundred men in ghastly
    death,
The four daughters, stretched on the marble pave-
    ment, silent, all
Fallen by the pestilence,—the rest moped round in
    guilty fears ;
And all the children in their beds were cut off in one
    night.
Thirty of Tiriel's sons remained, to wither in the palace—
Desolate, loathed, dumb, astonished—waiting for
    black death.

6.

And Hela led her father through the silence of the
    night,
Astonished, silent, till the morning beams began to
    spring.

" Now, Hela, I can go with pleasure, and dwell with
    Har and Heva,
Now that the curse shall clean devour all those guilty
    sons.
This is the right and ready way ; I know it by the
    sound
That our feet make. Remember, Hela, I have saved
    thee from death ;
Then be obedient to thy father, for the curse is taken
    off thee.
I dwelt with Myratana five years in the desolate rock ;
And all that time we waited for the fire to fall from
    heaven,
Or for the torrents of the sea to overwhelm you all.
But now my wife is dead, and all the time of grace is
    past.
You see the parent's curse. Now lead me where I
    have commanded."

" O leagued with evil spirits, thou accursed man of sin,—
True, I was born thy slave. Who asked thee to save
    me from death ?
'Twas for thyself, thou cruel man, because thou wantest
    eyes."

" True, Hela, this is the desert of all those cruel ones.
Is Tiriel cruel ? Look ! his daughter—and his young-
    est daughter—
Laughs at affection, glories in rebellion, scoffs at love.
I have not ate these two days ; lead me to Har and
    Heva's tent,
Or I will wrap thee up in such a terrible father's curse
That thou shalt feel worms in thy marrow creeping
    through thy bones ;

Yet thou shalt lead me. Lead me, I command, to
    Har and Heva."

" O cruel ! O destroyer ! O consumer ! O avenger !
To Har and Heva I will lead thee ; then would that
    they would curse,—
Then would they curse as thou hast cursed ! But
    they are not like thee !
O they are holy and forgiving, filled with loving
    mercy,
Forgetting the offences of their most rebellious children,
Or else thou wouldest not have lived to curse thy
    helpless children."

" Look on my eyes, Hela, and see (for thou hast eyes
    to see)
The tears swell from my stony fountains ; wherefore
    do I weep ?
Wherefore from my blind orbs art thou not seized
    with poisonous stings ?
Laugh, serpent, youngest venomous reptile of the
    flesh of Tiriel !
Laugh, for thy father Tiriel shall give thee cause to
    laugh,
Unless thou lead me to the tent of Har, child of the
    curse ! "

" Silence thy evil tongue, thou murderer of thy help-
    less children
I lead thee to the tent of Har : not that I mind thy
    curse,
But that I feel they will curse thee, and hang upon
    thy bones
Fell shaking agonies, and in each wrinkle of that face

Plant worms of death to feast upon the tongue or
    terrible curses ! ''

" Hela, my daughter, listen !   Thou art the daughter
    of Tiriel.
Thy father calls.   Thy father lifts his hand unto the
    heavens,
For thou hast laughed at my tears, and cursed thy
    aged father :
Let snakes rise from thy bedded locks, and laugh
    among thy curls ! ''

He ceased.   Her dark hair upright stood, while snakes
    infolded round
Her madding brows : her shrieks appalled the soul
    of Tiriel.

" What have I done, Hela, my daughter ?   Fear'st
    thou now the curse,
Or wherefore dost thou cry ?   Ah, wretch, to curse
    thy aged father !
Lead me to Har and Heva, and the curse of Tiriel
Shall fail.   If thou refuse, howl in the desolate moun-
    tains.''

7.

She, howling, led him over mountains and through
    frighted vales,
Till to the caves of Zazel they approached at eventide.

Forth from their caves old Zazel and his sons ran,
    when they saw
Their tyrant prince blind, and his daughter howling
    and leading him.

They laughed and mocked; some threw dirt and
    stones as they passed by.
But, when Tiriel turned around and raised his awful
    voice,
Some fled away; but Zazel stood still, and thus be-
    gan :—

"Bald tyrant, wrinkled cunning, listen to Zazel's
    chains ;
'Twas thou that chained thy brother Zazel ! Where
    are now thine eyes ?
Shout, beautiful daughter of Tiriel ; thou singest a
    sweet song !
Where are you going ? Come and eat some roots,
    and drink some water.
Thy crown is bald, old man ; the sun will dry thy
    brains away,
And thou wilt be as foolish as thy foolish brother
    Zazel."

The blind man heard, and smote his breast, and trem-
    bling passed on.
They threw dirt after them, till to the covert of a
    wood
The howling maiden led her father, where wild beasts
    resort,
Hoping to end her woes ; but from her cries the tigers
    fled.
All night they wandered through the wood ; and,
    when the sun arose,
They entered on the mountains of Har. At noon the
    happy tents
Were frighted by the dismal cries of Hela on the
    mountains.

But Har and Heva slept fearless as babes on loving
    breasts.

Mnetha awoke ; she ran and stood at the tent-door,
    and saw

The aged wanderer led towards the tents. She took
    her bow,

And chose her arrows, then advanced to meet the
    terrible pair.

8.

And Mnetha hasted, and met them at the gate of
    the lower garden.

" Stand still, or from my bow receive a sharp and
    winged death ! "

Then Tiriel stood, saying : " What soft voice threatens
    such bitter things ?

Lead me to Har and Heva ; I am Tiriel, King of the
    West."

And Mnetha led them to the tent of Har ; and Har
    and Heva

Ran to the door. When Tiriel felt the ankles of aged
    Har,

He said : " O weak mistaken father of a lawless race,

Thy laws, O Har, and Tiriel's wisdom, end together
    in a curse.

Why is one law given to the lion and the patient ox,

And why men bound beneath the heavens in a reptile
    form,

A worm of sixty winters creeping on the dusty ground ?

The child springs from the womb ; the fatner ready
    stands to form

The infant head, while the mother idly plays with
    her dog on her couch.

The young bosom is cold for lack of mother's nour-
　　ishment, and milk
Is cut off from the weeping mouth with difficulty and
　　pain.
The little lids are lifted, and the little nostrils opened;
The father forms a whip to rouse the sluggish senses
　　to act,
And scourges off all youthful fancies from the new-
　　born man.
Then walks the weak infant in sorrow, compelled to
　　number footsteps
Upon the sand.　And, when the drone has reached
　　his crawling length,
Black berries appear that poison all round him.　Such
　　was Tiriel,—
Compelled to pray repugnant and to humble the
　　immortal spirit,
Till I am subtle as a serpent in a paradise,
Consuming all—both flowers and fruits, insects and
　　warbling birds.
And now my paradise is fallen, and a drear sandy
　　plain
Returns my thirsty hissings in a curse on thee, O Har.
Mistaken father of a lawless race!—My voice is past."

He ceased, outstretched at Har and Heva's feet in
　　awful death.

THE BOOK OF THEL

THEL'S MOTTO

Does the Eagle know what is in the pit
  Or wilt thou go ask the Mole?
Can wisdom be put in a silver rod,
  Or love in a golden bowl?

I.

THE Daughters of [the] Seraphim led round their
  sunny flocks—
All but the youngest : she in paleness sought the secret
  air,
To fade away like morning beauty from her mortal day.
Down by the river of Adona her soft voice is heard,
And thus her gentle lamentation falls like morning dew.
" O life of this our Spring ! why fades the lotus of the
  water ?
Why fade these children of the Spring, born but to
  smile and fall ?
Ah ! Thel is like a watery bow, and like a parting
  cloud,
Like a reflection in a glass, like shadows in the water,
Like dreams of infants, like a smile upon an infant's
  face,
Like the dove's voice, like transient day, like music
  in the air.
Ah ! gentle may I lay me down, and gentle rest my head,
And gentle sleep the sleep of death, and gentle hear
  the voice
Of Him that walketh in the garden in the evening
  time ! "

The Lily of the Valley, breathing in the humble grass,
Answered the lovely maid, and said : " I am a watery
      weed,
And I am very small, and love to dwell in lowly vale ;
So weak, the gilded butterfly scarce perches on my
      head.
Yet I am visited from heaven ; and He that smiles
      on all
Walks in the valley, and each morn over me spreads
      His hand,
Saying, ' Rejoice, thou humble grass, thou new-born
      lily-flower,
Thou gentle maid of silent valleys and of modest
      brooks ;
For thou shalt be clothed in light and fed with morn-
      ing manna,
Till summer's heat melts thee beside the fountains
      and the springs,
To flourish in eternal vales.'   Then why should Thel
      complain ?
Why should the mistress of the vales of Har utter a
      sigh ? "
She ceased, and smiled in tears, then sat down in her
      silver shrine.

Thel answered : " O thou little virgin of the peace-
      ful valley,
Giving to those that cannot crave, the voiceless, the
      o'ertired :
Thy breath doth nourish the innocent lamb ; he smells
      thy milky garments,
He crops thy flowers, while thou sittest smiling in
      his face,

Wiping his mild and meekin mouth from all contagious
taints.

Thy wine doth purify the golden honey ; thy perfume,

Which thou dost scatter on every little blade of grass
that springs,

Revives the milkèd cow, and tames the fire-breathing
steed.

But Thel is like a faint cloud kindled at the rising sun :

I vanish from my pearly throne, and who shall find
my place ? "

" Queen of the vales ", the Lily answered, " ask the
tender Cloud,

And it shall tell thee why it glitters in the morning
sky,

And why it scatters its bright beauty through the
humid air.

Descend, O little Cloud, and hover before the eyes of
Thel."

The Cloud descended ; and the Lily bowed her modest
head,

And went to mind her numerous charge among the
verdant grass.

2.

" O little Cloud ", the virgin said, " I charge thee tell
to me

Why thou complainest not, when in one hour thou
fad'st away :

Then we shall seek thee, but not find. Ah ! Thel
is like to thee—

I pass away ; yet I complain, and no one hears my
voice."

The Cloud then showed his golden head, and his bright
    form emerged
Hovering and glittering on the air, before the face of
    Thel.
" O virgin, know'st thou not our steeds drink of the
    golden springs
Where Luvah doth renew his horses ? Look'st thou
    on my youth,
And fearest thou because I vanish and am seen no
    more ?
Nothing remains. O maid, I tell thee, when I pass
    away,
It is to tenfold life, to love, to peace, and raptures
    holy.
Unseen descending weigh my light wings upon
    balmy flowers,
And court the fair-eyed Dew to take me to her shining
    tent :
The weeping virgin trembling kneels before the risen
    sun,
Till we arise, linked in a golden band, and never part,
But walk united, bearing food to all our tender flowers."

" Dost thou, O little Cloud ? I fear that I am not
    like thee ;
For I walk through the vales of Har, and smell the
    sweetest flowers,
But I feed not the little flowers : I hear the warbling
    birds,
But I feed not the warbling birds, they fly and seek
    their food.
But Thel delights in these no more ! because I fade
    away,

And all shall say, ' Without a use this shining woman
    lived ;
Or did she only live to be at death the food of worms ? ' "

The Cloud reclined upon his airy throne, and answered
    thus :

" Then if thou art the food of worms, O virgin of the
    skies,
How great thy use, how great thy blessing ! Every
    thing that lives
Lives not alone nor for itself.   Fear not, and I will call
The weak Worm from its lowly bed, and thou shalt
    hear its voice.
Come forth, Worm of the silent valley, to thy pensive
    queen."

The helpless Worm arose, and sat upon the Lily's
    leaf,
And the bright Cloud sailed on to find his partner in
    the vale.

3.

Then Thel, astonished, viewed the Worm upon its
    dewy bed.
" Art thou a worm, image of weakness ? art thou but
    a worm ?
I see thee, like an infant, wrapped in the Lily's leaf.
Ah ! weep not, little voice ; thou canst not speak,
    but thou canst weep.
Is this a worm ?   I see thee lay helpless and naked,
    weeping,
And none to answer, none to cherish thee with mother's
    smiles."

The Clod of Clay heard the Worm's voice, and raised
　　her pitying head :

She bowed over the weeping infant, and her life ex-
　　haled

In milky fondness : then on Thel she fixed her humble
　　eyes.

" O beauty of the vales of Har ! we live not for our-
　　selves.

Thou seest me, the meanest thing, and so I am indeed·

My bosom of itself is cold, and of itself is dark ;

But He that loves the lowly pours His oil upon my
　　head,

And kisses me, and binds His nuptial bands around
　　my breast,

And says : ' Thou mother of my children, I have
　　loved thee,

And I have given thee a crown that none can take
　　away.'

But how this is, sweet maid, I know not, and I cannot
　　know :

I ponder, and I cannot ponder : yet I live and love ! "

The Daughter of Beauty wiped her pitying tears with
　　her white veil,

And said ; " Alas ! I knew not this, and therefore did
　　I weep.

That God would love a worm I knew, and punish the
　　evil foot

That wilful bruised its helpless form ; but that He
　　cherished it

With milk and oil I never knew, and therefore did I
　　weep.

And I complained in the mild air, because I fade away,

And lay me down in thy cold bed, and leave my shin-
    ing lot."

" Queen of the vales", the matron Clay answered,
    " I heard thy sighs,
And all thy moans flew o'er my roof, but I have called
    them down.
Wilt thou, O queen, enter my house ? 'Tis given
    thee to enter,
And to return : fear nothing, enter with thy virgin
    feet."

4.

The eternal gates' terrific Porter lifted the northern
    bar ;

Thel entered in, and saw the secrets of the land un-
    known.
She saw the couches of the dead, and where the fibrous
    root
Of every heart on earth infixes deep its restless twists :
A land of sorrows and of tears, where never smile was
    seen.

She wandered in the land of clouds, through valleys
    dark, listening
Dolours and lamentations : waiting oft beside a
    dewy grave,
She stood in silence, listening to the voices of the
    ground,
Till to her own grave-plot she came, and there she
    sat down,
And heard this voice of sorrow breathed from the hollow
    pit.

" Why cannot the ear be closed to its own destruction ?
Or the glistening eye to the poison of a smile ?
Why are eyelids stored with arrows ready drawn,
Where a thousand fighting-men in ambush lie,
Or an eye of gifts and graces showering fruits and
    coined gold ?
Why a tongue impressed with honey from every wind ?
Why an ear, a whirlpool fierce to draw creations in ?
Why a nostril wide inhaling terror, trembling, and
    affright ?
Why a tender curb upon the youthful burning boy ?
Why a little curtain of flesh on the bed of our desire ? "

The Virgin started from her seat, and with a shriek
Fled back unhindered till she came into the vales of
    Har.

———

THE MARRIAGE OF HEAVEN AND HELL

THE ARGUMENT

RINTRAH roars and shakes his fires in the burdened air,
Hungry clouds swag on the deep.

Once meek and in a perilous path
The just man kept his course along
The Vale of Death.
Roses are planted where thorns grow,
And on the barren heath
Sing the honey bees.

Then the perilous path was planted,
And a river and a spring
On every cliff and tomb,
And on the bleached bones

Red clay brought forth:
Till the villain left the paths of ease
To walk in perilous paths, and drive
The just man into barren climes.

Now the sneeking serpent walks
In mild humility;
And the just man rages in the wilds
Where lions roam.

Rintrah roars and shakes his fires in the burdened air,
Hungry clouds swag on the deep.

As a new heaven is begun, and it is now thirty-three
years since its advent, the eternal hell revives. And
lo! Swedenborg is the angel sitting at the tomb: his
writings are the linen clothes folded up. Now is the
dominion of Edom, and the return of Adam into Para-
dise.—See Isaiah xxxiv. and xxxv. chap.

Without contraries is no progression. Attraction
and repulsion, reason and energy, love and hate, are
necessary to human existence.

From these contraries spring what the religious call
good and evil. Good is the passive that obeys reason;
evil is the active springing from energy.

Good is heaven. Evil is hell.

THE VOICE OF THE DEVIL

ALL Bibles or sacred codes have been the cause of the
following errors;—

1. That man has two real existing principles, viz.,
a body and a soul.

2. That energy, called evil, is alone from the body;
and that reason, called good, is alone from the soul.

3. That God will torment man in eternity for following his energies.

But the following contraries to these are true :—

1. Man has no body distinct from his soul. For that called body is a portion of soul discerned by the five senses, the chief inlets of soul in this age.

2. Energy is the only life, and is from the body ; and reason is the bound or outward circumference of energy.

3. Energy is eternal delight.

Those who restrain desire, do so because theirs is weak enough to be restrained ; and the restrainer or reason usurps its place and governs the unwilling.

And being restrained, it by degrees becomes passive, till it is only the shadow of desire.

The history of this is written in Paradise Lost, and the Governor or Reason is called Messiah.

And the original archangel or possessor of the command of the heavenly host is called the Devil, or Satan, and his children are called Sin and Death.

But in the book of Job, Milton's Messiah is called Satan.

For this history has been adopted by both parties.

It indeed appeared to reason as if desire was cast out, but the Devil's account is, that the Messiah fell, and formed a heaven of what he stole from the abyss.

This is shown in the Gospel, where he prays to the Father to send the Comforter or desire that reason may have ideas to build on, the Jehovah of the Bible being no other than he who dwells in flaming fire. Know that after Christ's death he became Jehovah.

But in Milton, the Father is destiny, the Son a ratio of the five senses, and the Holy Ghost vacuum !

Note.—The reason Milton wrote in fetters when he wrote of angels and God, and at liberty when of devils and hell, is because he was a true poet, and of the devil's party without knowing it.

A MEMORABLE FANCY

As I was walking among the fires of hell, delighted with the enjoyments of genius, which to angels look like torment and insanity, I collected some of their proverbs, thinking that as the sayings used in a nation mark its character, so the proverbs of hell show the nature of infernal wisdom better than any description or buildings or garments.

When I came home, on the abyss of the five senses, where a flat-sided steep frowns over the present world, I saw a mighty devil folded in black clouds hovering on the sides of the rock ; with corroding fires he wrote the following sentence now perceived by the minds of men, and read by them on earth :—

"How do you know but every bird that cuts the airy way
Is an immense world of delight, closed by your senses five ? "

PROVERBS OF HELL

In seed-time learn, in harvest teach, in winter enjoy.

Drive your cart and your plough over the bones of the dead.

The road of excess leads to the palace of wisdom.

Prudence is a rich ugly old maid courted by Incapacity.

He who desires, but acts not, breeds pestilence.

The cut worm forgives the plough.

Dip him in the river who loves water.

A fool sees not the same tree that a wise man sees.

He whose face gives no light shall never become a star.

Eternity is in love with the productions of time.

The busy bee has no time for sorrow.

The hours of folly are measured by the clock, but of wisdom no clock can measure.

All wholesome food is caught without a net or a trap.

Bring out number, weight, and measure in a year of dearth.

No bird soars too high if he soars with his own wings.

A dead body revenges not injuries.

The most sublime act is to set another before you.

If the fool would persist in his folly he would become wise.

Folly is the cloak of knavery.

Shame is pride's cloak.

Prisons are built with stones of law, brothels with bricks of religion.

The pride of the peacock is the glory of God.

The lust of the goat is the bounty of God.

The wrath of the lion is the wisdom of God.

The nakedness of woman is the work of God.

Excess of sorrow laughs, excess of joy weeps.

The roaring of lions, the howling of wolves, the raging of the stormy sea, and the destructive sword are portions of eternity too great for the eye of man.

The fox condemns the trap, not himself.

Joys impregnate, sorrows bring forth.

Let man wear the fell of the lion, woman the fleece of the sheep.

The bird a nest, the spider a web, man friendship.

The selfish smiling fool and the sullen frowning fool shall be both thought wise that they may be a rod.

What is now proved was once only imagined.

The rat, the mouse, the fox, the rabbit watch the roots ; the lion, the tiger, the horse, the elephant watch the fruits.

The cistern contains, the fountain overflows.

One thought fills immensity.

Always be ready to speak your mind, and a base man will avoid you.

Everything possible to be believed is an image of truth.

The eagle never lost so much time as when he submitted to learn of the crow.

The fox provides for himself, but God provides for the lion.

Think in the morning, act in the noon, eat in the evening, sleep in the night.

He who has suffered you to impose on him knows you.

As the plough follows words, so God rewards prayers.

The tigers of wrath are wiser than the horses of instruction.

Expect poison from the standing water.

You never know what is enough unless you know what is more than enough.

Listen to the fool's reproach ; it is a kingly title.

The eyes of fire, the nostrils of air, the mouth of water the beard of earth.

The weak in courage is strong in cunning.

The apple tree never asks the beech how he shall grow, nor the lion the horse how he shall take his prey.

The thankful receiver bears a plentiful harvest.

If others had not been foolish we should have been so.

The soul of sweet delight can never be defiled.

When thou seest an eagle, thou seest a portion of genius. Lift up thy head !

As the caterpillar chooses the fairest leaves to lay her eggs on, so the priest lays his curse on the fairest joys.

To create a little flower is the labour of ages.

Damn braces, bless relaxes.

The best wine is the oldest, the best water the newest.

Prayers plough not ; praises reap not ; joys laugh not ; sorrows weep not.

The head sublime, the heart pathos, the genitals beauty, the hands and feet proportion.

As the air to a bird, or the sea to a fish, so is contempt to the contemptible.

The crow wished everything was black ; the owl that everything was white.

Exuberance is beauty.

If the lion was advised by the fox, he would be cunning.

Improvement makes straight roads, but the crooked roads without improvement are roads of genius.

Sooner murder an infant in its cradle than nurse unacted desires.

Where man is not, nature is barren.

Truth can never be told so as to be understood and not be believed.

Enough! or too much.

**

The ancient poets animated all sensible objects with gods or geniuses, calling them by the names and adorning them with properties of woods, rivers, mountains, lakes, cities, nations, and whatever their enlarged and numerous senses could perceive. And particularly they studied the genius of each city and country, placing it under its mental deity. Till a system was formed, which some took advantage of and enslaved the vulgar by attempting to realize or abstract the mental deities from their objects. Thus began priesthood. Choosing forms of worship from poetic tales. And at length they pronounced that the gods had ordered such things. Thus men forgot that all deities reside in the human breast.

A MEMORABLE FANCY

The Prophets Isaiah and Ezekiel dined with me, and I asked them how they dared so roundly to assert that God spoke to them, and whether they did not think at the time that they would be misunderstood, and so be the cause of imposition.

Isaiah answered: " I saw no God, nor heard any, in a finite organical perception : but my senses discovered the infinite in everything ; and as I was then persuaded, and remain confirmed, that the voice of honest indignation is the voice of God, I cared not for consequences, but wrote."

Then I asked : " Does a firm persuasion that a thing is so, make it so ? "

He replied : " All poets believe that it does, and in ages of imagination this firm persuasion removed mountains ; but many are not capable of a firm persuasion of anything."

Then Ezekiel said : " The philosophy of the East taught the first principles of human perception ; some nations held one principle for the origin, and some another. We of Israel taught that the poetic genius (as you now call it) was the first principle, and all the others merely derivative, which was the cause of our despising the priests and philosophers of other countries, and prophesying that all gods would at last be proved to originate in ours, and to be the tributaries of the poetic genius. It was this that our great poet King David desired so fervently, and invokes so pathetically, saying by this he conquers enemies and governs kingdoms ; and we so loved our God that we cursed in His name all the deities of surrounding nations, and asserted that they had rebelled. From these opinions the vulgar came to think that all nations would at last be subject to the Jews.

" This ", said he, " like all firm persuasions, is come to pass, for all nations believe the Jews' code, and worship the Jews' God ; and what greater subjection can be ? "

I heard this with some wonder, and must confess my own conviction. After dinner I asked Isaiah to favour the world with his lost works ; he said none of equal value was lost. Ezekiel said the same of his.

I also asked Isaiah what made him go naked and barefoot three years. He answered, " 'The same that made our friend Diogenes the Grecian."

I then asked Ezekiel why he ate dung, and lay so

long on his right and left side. He answered, "The desire of raising other men into a perception of the infinite. This the North American tribes practise. And is he honest who resists his genius or conscience, only for the sake of present ease or gratification?"

***

The ancient tradition that the world will be consumed in fire at the end of six thousand years is true, as I have heard from hell.

For the cherub with his flaming sword is hereby commanded to leave his guard at [the] tree of life, and when he does, the whole creation will be consumed and appear infinite and holy, whereas it now appears finite and corrupt.

This will come to pass by an improvement of sensual enjoyment.

But first the notion that man has a body distinct from his soul is to be expunged; this I shall do, by printing in the infernal method by corrosives, which in hell are salutary and medicinal, melting apparent surfaces away, and displaying the infinite which was hid.

If the doors of perception were cleansed, everything would appear to man as it is, infinite.

For the man has closed himself up, till he sees all things through narrow chinks of his cavern.

A MEMORABLE FANCY

I was in a printing-house in hell, and saw the method in which knowledge is transmitted from generation to generation.

In the first chamber was a dragon-man, clearing

away the rubbish from a cave's mouth; within, a number of dragons were hollowing the cave.

In the second chamber was a viper folding round the rock and the cave, and others adorning it with silver, gold, and precious stones.

In the third chamber was an eagle with wings and feathers of air; he caused the inside of the cave to be infinite; around were numbers of eagle-like men, who built palaces in the immense cliffs.

In the fourth chamber were lions of flaming fire raging around and melting the metals into living fluids.

In the fifth chamber were unnamed forms, which cast the metals into the expanse.

There they were received by men who occupied the sixth chamber, and took the forms of books, and were arranged in libraries.

**

The giants who formed this world into its sensual existence, and now seem to live in it in chains, are in truth the causes of its life and the sources of all activity, but the chains are the cunning of weak and tame minds, which have power to resist energy, according to the proverb, " The weak in courage is strong in cunning."

Thus one portion of being is the Prolific, the other the Devouring; to the devourer it seems as if the producer was in his chains; but it is not so, he only takes portions of existence, and fancies that the whole.

But the Prolific would cease to be prolific unless the Devourer as a sea received the excess of his delights.

Some will say, " Is not God alone the Prolific ? " I answer, " God only acts and is in existing beings or men."

These two classes of men are always upon earth, and they should be enemies : whoever tries to reconcile them seeks to destroy existence.

Religion is an endeavour to reconcile the two.

NOTE.—Jesus Christ did not wish to unite but to separate them, as in the parable of sheep and goats ; and He says : " I came not to send peace, but a sword."

Messiah, or Satan, or Tempter, was formerly thought to be one of the antediluvians who are our energies.

A MEMORABLE FANCY

AN Angel came to me and said : " O pitiable foolish young man ! O horrible, O dreadful state ! consider the hot burning dungeon thou art preparing for thyself to all eternity, to which thou art going in such career."

I said . " Perhaps you will be willing to show me my eternal lot, and we will contemplate together upon it, and see whether your lot or mine is most desirable."

So he took me through a stable, and through a church, and down into the church vault, at the end of which was a mill ; through the mill we went, and came to a cave, down the winding cavern we groped our tedious way, till a void boundless as a nether sky appeared beneath us, and we held by the roots of trees, and hung over this immensity ; but I said : " If you please, we will commit ourselves to this void, and see whether Providence is here also ; if you will not, I will." But he answered : " Do not presume, O young man ; but as we here remain, behold thy lot, which will soon appear when the darkness passes away."

So I remained with him sitting in the twisted root of

an oak ; he was suspended in a fungus, which hung with the head downward into the deep.

By degrees we beheld the infinite abyss, fiery as the smoke of a burning city ; beneath us at an immense distance was the sun, black but shining ; round it were fiery tracks on which revolved vast spiders. crawling after their prey, which flew, or rather swum, in the infinite deep, in the most terrific shapes of animals sprung from corruption ; and the air was full of them, and seemed composed of them. These are devils, and are called powers of the air. I now asked my companion which was my eternal lot. He said : " Between the black and white spiders."

But now, from between the black and white spiders a cloud and fire burst and rolled through the deep, blackening all beneath so that the nether deep grew black as a sea, and rolled with a terrible noise. Beneath us was nothing now to be seen but a black tempest, till looking East between the clouds and the waves, we saw a cataract of blood mixed with fire, and not many stones' throw from us appeared and sunk again the scaly fold of a monstrous serpent. At last to the East, distant about three degrees, appeared a fiery crest above the waves ; slowly it reared like a ridge of golden rocks, till we discovered two globes of crimson fire, from which the sea fled away in clouds of smoke ; and now we saw it was the head of Leviathan ; his forehead was divided into streaks of green and purple, like those on a tiger's forehead ; soon we saw his mouth and red gills hang just above the raging foam, tinging the black deeps with beams of blood, advancing toward us with all the fury of a spiritual existence.

My friend the Angel climbed up from his station into the mill. I remained alone, and then this appearance was no more, but I found myself sitting on a pleasant bank beside a river by moonlight, hearing a harper who sung to the harp ; and his theme was : "The man who never alters his opinion is like standing water, and breeds reptiles of the mind."

But I arose, and sought for the mill, and there I found my Angel, who, surprised, asked me how I escaped.

I answered : "All that we saw was owing to your metaphysics ; for when you ran away, I found myself on a bank by moonlight, hearing a harper. But now we have seen my eternal lot, shall I show you yours ? " He laughed at my proposal ; but I by force suddenly caught him in my arms, and flew Westerly through the night, till we were elevated above the earth's shadow ; then I flung myself with him directly into the body of the sun ; here I clothed myself in white, and taking in my hand Swedenborg's volumes, sunk from the glorious clime, and passed all the planets till we came to Saturn. Here I stayed to rest, and then leaped into the void, between Saturn and the fixed stars.

"Here," said I, "is your lot ; in this space, if space it may be called." Soon we saw the stable and the church, and I took him to the altar and opened the Bible, and lo ! it was a deep pit, into which I descended, driving the Angel before me. Soon we saw seven houses of brick, one we entered ; in it were a number of monkeys, baboons, and all of that species, chained by the middle, grinning and snatching at one another, but withheld by the shortness of their chains. However, I saw that they sometimes grew numerous, and then the weak were caught by the strong, and with a grinning aspect, first coupled with and then devoured by plucking off first one limb and then another till the body was left a helpless trunk ; this, after grinning and kissing it with seeming fondness, they devoured too. And here and there I saw one savourily picking the flesh off his own tail. As the stench terribly annoyed us both, we went into the mill; and I in my hand brought the skeleton of a body, which in the mill was Aristotle's Analytics.

So the Angel said : " Thy phantasy has imposed upon me, and thou oughtest to be ashamed."

I answered : " We impose on one another, and it is but lost time to converse with you whose works are only Analytics."

**

" I have always found that angels have the vanity to speak of themselves as the only wise ; this they do with a confident insolence sprouting from systematic reasoning.

" Thus Swedenborg boasts that what he writes is new ; though it is only the contents or index of already published books.

" A man carried a monkey about for a show, and because he was a little wiser than the monkey, grew vain, and conceived himself as much wiser than seven men. It is so with Swedenborg : he shows the folly of churches, and exposes hypocrites, till he imagines that all are religious, and himself the single one on earth that ever broke a net.

" Now hear a plain fact : Swedenborg has not written

one new truth. Now hear another : he has written all the old falsehoods.

"And now hear the reason : he conversed with angels who are all religious, and conversed not with devils who all hate religion, for he was incapable through his conceited notions.

"Thus Swedenborg's writings are a recapitulation of all superficial opinions, and an analysis of the more sublime, but no further.

"Have now another plain fact : any man of mechanical talents may from the writings of Paracelsus or Jacob Behmen produce ten thousand volumes of equal value with Swedenborg's, and from those of Dante or Shakespeare an infinite number.

"But when he has done this, let him not say that he knows better than his master, for he only holds a candle in sunshine."

A MEMORABLE FANCY

ONCE I saw a Devil in a flame of fire, who arose before an Angel that sat on a cloud, and the Devil uttered these words : "The worship of God is, honouring His gifts in other men each according to his genius, and loving the greatest men best. Those who envy or calumniate great men hate God, for there is no other God."

The Angel hearing this became almost blue, but mastering himself he grew yellow, and at last white-pink and smiling, and then replied : "Thou idolater, is not God one ? and is not He visible in Jesus Christ ? and has not Jesus Christ given his sanction to the law of ten commandments ? and are not all other men fools, sinners, and nothings ? "

The Devil answered, " Bray a fool in a mortar with wheat, yet shall not his folly be beaten out of him. If Jesus Christ is the greatest man, you ought to love Him in the greatest degree.   Now hear how He has given His sanction to the law of ten commandments.   Did He not mock at the Sabbath, and so mock the Sabbath's God ? murder those who were murdered because of him ? turn away the law from the woman taken with adultery ? steal the labour of others to support Him ? bear false witness when He omitted making a defence before Pilate ? covet when He prayed for His disciples, and when He bid them shake off the dust of their feet against such as refused to lodge them ? I tell you, no virtue can exist without breaking these ten commandments.   Jesus was all virtue, and acted from impulse, not from rules."

When he had so spoken, I beheld the Angel, who stretched out his arms embracing the flame of fire, and he was consumed, and arose as Elijah.

NOTE.—This Angel, who is now become a Devil, is my particular friend ; we often read the Bible together in its infernal or diabolical sense, which the world shall have if they behave well.

I have also the Bible of Hell, which the world shall have whether they will or no.

One law for the lion and ox is oppression.

A SONG OF LIBERTY

1. The eternal female groaned ; it was heard over all the earth :

2. Albion's coast is sick silent ; the American meadows faint.

3. Shadows of prophesy shiver along by the lakes

and the rivers, and mutter across the ocean. France, rend down thy dungeon!

4. Golden Spain, burst the barriers of old Rome!

5. Cast thy keys, O Rome, into the deep—down falling, even to eternity down falling;

6. And weep!

7. In her trembling hands she took the new-born terror, howling.

8. On those infinite mountains of light now barred out by the Atlantic sea, the new-born fire stood before the starry king.

9. Flagged with grey-browed snows and thunderous visages, the jealous wings waved over the deep.

10. The speary hand burned aloft; unbuckled was the shield; forth went the hand of jealousy among the flaming hair, and hurled the new-born wonder through the starry night.

11. The fire, the fire is falling!

12. Look up! look up! O citizen of London, enlarge thy countenance! O Jew, leave counting gold: return to thy oil and wine! O African, black African! (Go, winged thought, widen his forehead.)

13. The fiery limbs, the flaming hair shot like the sinking sun into the Western sea.

14. Waked from his eternal sleep, the hoary element roaring fled away.

15. Down rushed beating his wings in vain the jealous king, his grey-browed councillors, thunderous warriors, curled veterans; among helms and shields, and chariots, horses, elephants, banners, castles, slings, and rocks.

16. Falling, rushing, ruining, buried in the ruins, on Urthona's dens.

17. All night beneath the ruins, then their sullen flames, faded, emerge round the gloomy king.

18. With thunder and fire, leading his starry hosts through the waste wilderness, he promulgates his ten commands, glancing his beamy eyelids over the deep in dark dismay,

19. Where the Son of Fire in his Eastern cloud, while the Morning plumes her golden breast,

20. Spurning the clouds written with curses, stamps the stony law to dust, loosing the eternal horses from the dens of night, crying: "Empire is no more! and now the lion and wolf shall cease."

CHORUS.

Let the priests of the raven of dawn, no longer in deadly black, with hoarse note curse the sons of joy. Nor his accepted brethren whom, tyrant, he calls free, lay the bound or build the roof. Nor pale religious lechery call that virginity that wishes, but acts not!

For everything that lives is holy.

VISIONS OF THE DAUGHTERS OF ALBION
The eye sees more than the heart knows.

THE ARGUMENT.

I LOVED Theotormon,
And I was not ashamed;
I trembled in my virgin fears,
And I hid in Leutha's vale.

I plucked Leutha's flower,
And I rose up from the vale;
But the terrible thunders tore
My virgin mantle in twain.

VISIONS.

ENSLAVED, the Daughters of Albion weep : a trembling
lamentation
Upon their mountains ; in their valleys, sighs towards
America.

For the soft soul of America, Oothoon wandered in
woe,
Along the vales of Leutha seeking flowers to comfort
her ;
And thus she spoke to the bright Marygold of Leutha's
vale :

" Art thou a flower ? art thou a nymph ?   I see thee
now a flower
Now a nymph ! I dare not pluck thee from thy
dewy bed."

The golden nymph replied : " Pluck thou my flower.
Oothoon the mild,
Another flower shall spring, because the soul of sweet
delight
Can never pass away." She ceased and closed her
golden shrine.

Then Oothoon plucked the flower, saying : " I pluck
thee from thy bed,
Sweet flower, and put thee here to glow between my
breasts ;
And thus I turn my face to where my whole soul seeks."

Over the waves she went in winged exulting swift
delight,
And over Theotormon's reign took her impetuous
course.

Bromion rent her with his thunders; on his stormy
 bed
Lay the faint maid, and soon her woes appalled his
 thunders hoarse.

Bromion spoke: "Behold this harlot here on Bro-
 mion's bed,
And let the jealous dolphins sport around the lovely
 maid!
Thy soft American plains are mine, and mine thy
 north and south;
Stamped with my signet are the swarthy children of
 the sun;
They are obedient, they resist not, they obey the
 scourge;
Their daughters worship terrors and obey the violent.
Now thou may'st marry Bromion's harlot, and protect
 the child
Of Bromion's rage, that Oothoon shall put forth in
 nine moons' time."

Then storms rent Theotormon's limbs; he rolled his
 waves around,
And folded his black jealous waters round the adul-
 terate pair.
Bound back to back in Bromion's caves terror and
 meekness dwell.

At entrance Theotormon sits, wearing the threshold
 hard
With secret tears; beneath him sound like waves on
 a desert shore
The voice of slaves beneath the sun, and children
 bought with money,

That shiver in religious caves beneath the burning
    fires
Of lust, that belch incessant from the summits of the
    earth.

Oothoon weeps not : she cannot weep !—her tears
    are locked up.
But she can howl incessant, writhing her soft snowy
    limbs,
And calling Theotormon's eagles to prey upon her
    flesh :
I call with holy voice : kings of the sounding air,
Rend away this defiled bosom that I may reflect
The image of Theotormon on my pure transparent
    breast.

The eagles at her call descend and rend their bleeding
    prey.
Theotormon severely smiles ; her soul reflects the
    smile,
As the clear spring muddied with feet of beasts grows
    pure and smiles.
The Daughters of Albion hear her woes, and echo
    back her sighs :

" Why does my Theotormon sit weeping upon the
    threshold ?
And Oothoon hovers by his side, persuading him in
    vain.
I cry, Arise, O Theotormon, for the village dog
Barks at the breaking day, the nightingale has done
    lamenting,
The lark does rustle in the ripe corn, and the eagle
    returns

From nightly prey, and lifts his golden beak to the
pure east,
Shaking the dust from his immortal pinions to awake
The sun that sleeps too long.   Arise, my Theotormon,
I am pure ;
Because the night is gone that closed me in its deadly
black.
They told me that the night and day were all that I
could see ;
They told me that I had five senses to inclose me up ;
And they inclosed my infinite brain into a narrow
circle,
And sunk my heart into the abyss, a red round globe
hot burning,
Till all from life I was obliterated and erased.
Instead of morn arises a bright shadow, like an eye
In the eastern cloud ; instead of night a sickly charnel
house.
That Theotormon hears me not ! To him the night
and morn
Are both alike : a sight of sighs, a morning of fresh
tears.
And none but Bromion can hear my lamentations.

" With what sense is it that the chicken shuns the
ravenous hawk ?
With what sense does the tame pigeon measure out
the expanse ?
With what sense does the bee form cells ? Have not
the mouse and frog
Eyes and ears and sense of touch ? yet are their habi-
tations
And their pursuits as different as their forms and as
their joys.

Ask the wild ass why he refuses burdens, and the
    meek camel
Why he loves man. Is it because of eye, ear, mouth,
    or skin,
Or breathing nostrils ? No, for these the wolf and
    tiger have.
Ask the blind worm the secrets of the grave, and why
    her spires
Love to curl round the bones of death ; and ask the
    ravenous snake
Where she gets poison ; and the winged eagle why
    he loves the sun,—
And then tell me the thoughts of man, that have been
    hid of old.

" Silent I hover all the night, and all day could be
    silent,
If Theotormon once would turn his loved eyes upon
    me.
How can I be defiled when I reflect thy image pure ?
Sweetest the fruit that the worm feeds on, and the
    soul preyed on by woe,
The new washed lamb tinged with the village smoke,
    and the bright swan
By the red earth of our immortal river : I bathe my
    wings,
And I am white and pure to hover round Theotormon's
    breast."

Then Theotormon broke his silence, and he answered :

" Tell me what is the night or day to one o'erflowed
    with woe ?
Tell me what is a thought, and of what substance is
    it made ?

Tell me what is a joy, and in what gardens do joys
  grow ?
And in what rivers swim the sorrows ? and upon wha'
  mountains
Wave shadows of discontent ? and in what houses
  dwell the wretched,
Drunken with woe, forgotten, and shut up from cold
  despair ?

" Tell me where dwell the thoughts forgotten till thou
  call them forth ?
Tell me where dwell the joys of old ? and where the
  ancient loves ?
And when will they renew again, and the night of
  oblivion past ?
That I might traverse times and spaces far remote,
  and bring
Comforts into a present sorrow and a night of pain.
Where goest thou, O thought ? To what remote
  land is thy flight ?
If thou returnest to the present moment of affliction,
Wilt thou bring comforts on thy wings, and dews and
  honey and balm,
Or poison from the desert wilds, from the eyes of the
  envier ? "

Then Bromion said, and shook the cavern with his
  lamentation :

" Thou knowest that the ancient trees seen by thine
  eyes have fruit ;
But knowest thou that trees and fruits flourish upon
  the earth
To gratify senses unknown ?—trees, beasts, and birds
  unknown,

Unknown, not unperceived, spread in the infinite
    microscope,
In places yet unvisited by the voyager, and in worlds
Over another kind of seas, and in atmospheres un-
    known.
Ah ! are there other wars beside the wars of sword
    and fire ?
And are there other sorrows beside the sorrows of
    poverty ?
And are there other joys beside the joys of riches and
    ease ?
And is there not one law for both the lion and the ox ?
And is there not eternal fire and eternal chains
To bind the phantoms of existence from eternal life ? ' "

Then Oothoon waited silent all the day and all the
    night,
But when the morn arose, her lamentation renewed.
The Daughters of Albion hear her woes, and echo
    back her sighs.

" O Urizen, creator of men, mistaken demon of heaven !
Thy joys are tears, thy labour vain, to form men to
    thine image.
How can one joy absorb another ?   Are not different
    joys
Holy, eternal, infinite ; and each joy is a love ?

" Does not the great mouth laugh at a gift, and the
    narrow eyelids mock
At the labour that is above payment ? and wilt thou
    take the ape
For thy counsellor, or the dog for a schoolmaster to
    thy children ?

Does he who contemns poverty, and he who turns
    with abhorrence

From usury, feel the same passion, or are they moved
    alike ?

How can the giver of gifts experience the delights of
    the merchant ?

How the industrious citizen the pains of the husband-
    man ?

How different far the fat fed hireling with hollow drum,

Who buys whole cornfields into wastes, and sings
    upon the heath,

How different their eye and ear ! how different the
    world to them !

With what sense does the parson claim the labour of
    the farmer ?

What are his nets and gins and traps, and how does
    he surround him

With cold floods of abstraction, and with forests of
    solitude,

To build him castles and high spires, where kings and
    priests may dwell,

Till she who burns with youth, and knows no fixed
    lot, is bound

In spells of law to one she loaths ? And must she
    drag the chain

Of life in weary lust ? Must chilling, murderous
    thoughts obscure

The clear heaven of her eternal spring ; to bear the
    wintry rage

Of a harsh terror driven to madness, bound to hold
    a rod

Over her shrinking shoulders all the day, and all the
    night

To turn the wheel of false desire ; and longings that
    make her womb
To the abhorred birth of cherubs in the human form
That live a pestilence and die a meteor, and are no
    more ?
Till the child dwell with one he hates, and do the deed
    he loaths,
And the impure scourge force his seed into its unripe
    birth,
Ere yet his eyelids can behold the arrows of the day.

" Does the whale worship at thy footsteps as the
    hungry dog ?
Or does he scent the mountain prey, because his nos-
    trils wide
Draw in the ocean ?   Does his eye discern the flying
    cloud
As the raven's eye ? or does he measure the expanse
    like the vulture ?
Does the still spider view the cliffs where eagles hide
    their young ?
Or does the fly rejoice because the harvest is brought
    in ?
Does not the eagle scorn the earth, and despise the
    treasures beneath ?
But the mole knoweth what is there, and the worm
    shall tell it thee.
Does not the worm erect a pillar in the mouldering
    churchyard,
And a palace of eternity in the jaws of the hungry
    grave ?
Over his porch these words are written : ' Take thy
    bliss, O man !

And sweet shall be thy taste, and sweet thy infant
  joys renew ! '

" Infancy, fearless, lustful, happy, nestling for delight
In laps of pleasure !   Innocence, honest, open, seeking
The vigorous joys of morning light, open to virgin
  bliss !
Who taught thee modesty, subtile modesty ?   Child
  of night and sleep,
When thou awakest wilt thou dissemble all thy secret
  joys ?
Or wert thou not awake when all this mystery was
  disclosed ?
Then cam'st thou forth a modest virgin knowing to
  dissemble,
With nets found under thy night pillow to catch virgin
  joy,
And brand it with the name of whore ; and sell it in
  the night,
In silence, even without a whisper, and in seeming
  sleep.
Religious dreams and holy vespers, light thy smoky
  fires—
Once were thy fires lighted by the eyes of honest
  morn.
And does my Theotormon seek this hypocrite modesty ?
This knowing, artful, secret, fearful, cautious, tremb-
  ling hypocrite !
Then is Oothoon a whore indeed ! and all the virgin
  joys
Of life are harlots ; and Theotormon is a sick man's
  dream,
And Oothoon is the crafty slave of selfish holiness.

" But Oothoon is not so, a virgin filled with virgin
    fancies,
Open to joy and to delight wherever beauty appears.
If in the morning sun I find it, there my eyes are fixed
In happy copulation ; if in evening mild, wearied
    with work,
Sit on a bank and draw the pleasures of this free-
    born joy.

" The moment of desire ! the moment of desire ! The
    virgin
That pines for man shall awaken her womb to enor-
    mous joys,
In the secret shadows of her chamber ; the youth
    shut up from
The lustful joy shall forget to generate and create an
    amorous image
In the shadows of his curtains and in the folds of his
    silent pillow.
Are not these the places of religion, the rewards of
    continence,
The self-enjoyings of self-denial ? Why dost thou
    seek religion ?
Is it because acts are not lovely, that thou seekest
    solitude
Where the horrible darkness is impressed with reflec-
    tions of desire ?

" Father of Jealousy, be thou accursed from the
    earth !
Why hast thou taught my Theotormon this accursed
    thing !
Till beauty fades from off my shoulders, darkened
    and cast out.

A solitary shadow wailing on the margin of nonentity.

" I cry, Love ! Love ! Love ! happy, happy Love !
    free as the mountain wind !
Can that be Love that drinks another as a sponge
    drinks water,
That clouds with jealousy his night, with weepings
    all the day,
To spin a web of age around him grey and hoary
    dark,
Till his eyes sicken at the fruit that hangs before his
    sight ?
Such is self-love that envies all ; a creeping skeleton,
With lamplike eyes, watching around the frozen
    marriage bed.
But silken nets and traps of adamant will Oothoon
    spread,
And catch for thee girls of mild silver or of furious
    gold ;
I'll be beside thee on a bank, and view their wanton
    play
In lovely copulation, bliss on bliss with Theotormon.
Red as the rosy morning, lustful as the first-born
    beam,
Oothoon shall view his dear delight, nor e'er with
    jealous cloud
Come in the heaven of generous love, nor selfish blight
    ings bring.

" Does the sun walk in glorious raiment on the secret
    floor
Where the cold miser spreads his gold ?   Or does the
    bright cloud drop

On his stone threshold ; does his eye behold the beam that brings
Expansion to the eye of pity ?   Or will he bind himself
Beside the ox to thy hard furrow ?   Does not that mild beam blot
The bat, the owl, the glowing tiger, and the King of night ;
The sea-fowl takes the wintry blast for a cooling to her limbs,
And the wild snake the pestilence to adorn him with gems and gold.
And trees and birds and beasts and men behold their eternal joy.
Arise, you little glancing wings, and sing your infant joy :
Arise, and drink your bliss, for everything that lives is holy ! "

Thus every morning wails Oothoon, but Theotormon sits
Upon the margined ocean conversing with shadows dire.

The Daughters of Albion hear her woes, and echo back her sighs.

AHANIA.

CHAPTER I.

I.

FUZON on a chariot iron-winged,
On spiked flames rose : his hot visage

Flamed furious ; sparkles his hair and beard ;
Shot down his wide bosom and shoulders ;
On clouds of smoke rages his chariot,
And his right hand burns red in its cloud,
Moulding into a vast globe his wrath,
As the thunder-stone is moulded :
Son of Urizen's silent burnings.

2.

" Shall we worship this Demon of Smoke,"
Said Fuzon, " this abstract nonentity,
This cloudy God seated on waters,
Now seen, now obscured, King of Sorrow ? "

3.

So he spoke : in a fiery flame,
On Urizen frowning indignant,
The globe of wrath shaking on high.
Roaring with fury, he threw
The howling globe ! burning it flew,
Lengthening into a hungry beam.   Swiftly

4.

Opposed to the exulting flamed beam
The broad disc of Urizen, upheaved
Across the void many a mile.

5.

It was forged in mills where the winter
Beats incessant : ten winters the disc
Unremitting endured the cold hammer.

6.

But the strong arm that sent it remembered
The sounding beam : laughing it tore through
That beaten mass ; keeping its direction,
The cold loins of Urizen dividing.

7.

Dire shrieked his invisible lust,
Deep groaned Urizen. Stretching his awful hand,
Ahania (so name his parted soul)
He seized on his mountains of jealousy ;
He groaned anguished and called her Sin,
Kissing her and weeping over her,
Then hid her in darkness, in silence :
Jealous, though she was invisible.

8.

She fell down, a faint shadow wandering
In chaos, and circling dark Urizen,
As the moon anguished circles the earth,
Hopeless, abhorred, a death shadow !
Unseen, unbodied, unknown,
The mother of Pestilence.

9.

But the fiery beam of Fuzon
Was a pillar of fire to Egypt,
Five hundred years wandering on earth,
Till Los seized it and beat in a mass
With the body of the sun.

Chapter II.

1.

But the forehead of Urizen gathering,
And his eyes pale with anguish, his lips
Blue and changing, in tears and bitter
Contrition he prepared his bow,

2.

Formed of ribs, that in his dark solitude
When obscured in his forests fell monsters
Arose. For his dire contemplations
Rushed down like floods from his mountains
In torrents of mud, settling thick,
With eggs of unnatural production
Forthwith hatching ; some howled on his hills,
Some in vales, some aloft flew in air.

3.

Of these, an enormous dread serpent,
Scaled, and poisonous-horned,
Approached Urizen, even to his knees,
As he sat on his dark-rooted oak.

4.

With his horns he pushed furious.
Great the conflict and great the jealousy
In cold poisons ; but Urizen smote him.

5.

First he poisoned the rocks with his blood,
Then polished his ribs, and his sinews
Dried, laid them apart till winter ;
Then a bow black prepared ; on this bow

A poisoned rock placed in silence ;
He uttered these words to the bow :

6.

" O bow of the clouds of secrecy,
O nerve of that lust-formed monster.
Send this rock swift invisible through
The black clouds on the bosom of Fuzon ! "

7.

So saying, in torment of his wounds
He bent the enormous ribs slowly—
A circle of darkness ; then fixed
The sinew in its rest ; then the rock—
Poisonous source !—placed with art, lifting difficult
Its weighty bulk : silent the rock lay.

8.

While Fuzon his tigers unloosing
Thought Urizen slain by his wrath.
" I am God ", said he ; " eldest of things ! "

9.

Sudden sings the rock ; swift and invisible
On Fuzon flew, entered his bosom.
His beautiful visage, his tresses
That gave light to the mornings of heaven,
Were smitten with darkness, deformed,
And outstretched on the edge of the forest.

10.

But the rock fell upon the earth :
Mount Sinai, in Arabia.

CHAPTER III.

1.

The globe shook ; and Urizen seated
On black clouds his sore wound anointed.
The ointment flowed down on the void
Mixed with blood : here the snake gets her poison.

2.

With difficulty and great pain Urizen
Lifted on high the dead corse :
On his shoulders he bore it to where
A tree hung over the immensity.

3.

For when Urizen shrunk away
From eternals, he sat on a rock,
Barren ; a rock which he himself
From redounding fancies had petrified.
Many tears fell on the rock,
Many sparks of vegetation.
Soon shot the pained root
Of mystery under his heel ;
It grew a thick tree ; he wrote
In silence his book of iron :
Till the horrid plant, bending its boughs,
Grew to roots when it felt the earth,
And again sprung to many a tree.

4.

Amazed, started Urizen when
He beheld himself compassed round
And high-roofed over with trees.
He arose, but the stems stood so thick

He with difficulty and great pain
Brought his books, all but the book
Of iron, from the dismal shade.

5.

The tree still grows over the void,
Enrooting itself all around—
An endless labyrinth of woe!

6.

The corse of his first begotten
On the accursed tree of mystery,
On the topmost stem of this tree
Urizen nailed Fuzon's corse.

CHAPTER IV.

1.

Forth flew the arrows of pestilence
Round the pale-living corse on the tree.

2.

For in Urizen's slumbers of abstraction,
In the infinite ages of eternity:
When his nerves of joy melted and flowed
A white lake on the dark blue air,
In perturbed pain and dismal torment,
Now stretching out, now swift conglobing.

3.

Effluvia vapoured above
In noxious clouds: these hovered thick
Over the disorganized immortal,

Till petrific pain scurfed o'er the lakes
As the bones of man, solid and dark.

4.

The clouds of disease hovered wide
Around the immortal in torment.
Perching around the hurtling bones,
Disease on disease, shape on shape,
Winged, screaming in blood and torment.

5.

The eternal prophet beat on his anvils,
Enraged in the desolate darkness ;
He forged nets of iron around,
And Los threw them around the bones.

6.

The shapes, screaming, fluttered vain ;
Some combined into muscles and glands,
Some organs for craving and lust,
Most remained on the tormented void—
Urizen's army of horrors.

7.

Round the pale living corse on the tree
Forty years flew the arrows of pestilence

8.

Wailing, and terror, and woe
Ran through all his dismal world.
Forty years all his sons and daughters
Felt their skulls harden.   Then Asia
Arose in the pendulous deep,

9.

They reptilize upon the earth.

10.

Fuzon groaned on the tree.

Chapter V.

1.

The lamenting voice ot Ahania,
Weeping upon the void,
And round the tree of Fuzon,
Distant in solitary night,
Her voice was heard, but no form
Had she, but her tears from clouds
Eternal fell round the tree.

2.

And the voice cried : " Ah ! Urizen, love,
Flower of morning ! I weep on the verge
Of nonentity ! How wide the abyss
Between Ahania and thee !

3.

" I lie on the verge of the deep,
I see thy dark clouds ascend,
I see thy black forests and floods,
A horrible waste to my eyes.

4.

" Weeping I walk over the rocks,
Over dens and through valleys of death.
Why didst thou despise Ahania,
To cast me from thy bright presence
Into the world of loneness ?

5.

" I cannot touch his hand,
Nor weep on his knees, nor hear
His voice and bow, nor see his eyes
And joy, nor hear his footsteps ; and
My heart leap at the lovely sound !
I cannot kiss the place
Whereon his bright feet have trod.
But I wander on the rocks
With hard necessity.

6.

" Where is my golden palace ?
Where my ivory bed ?
Where the joy of my morning hour ?
Where the sons of eternity singing ?

7.

" To awake bright Urizen, my king,
To arise to the mountain sport ;
To the bliss of eternal valleys.

8.

" To awake my king in the morn,
To embrace Ahania's joy,
On the breath of his open bosom,
From my soft cloud of dew to fall
In showers of life on his harvests.

9.

" When he gave my happy soul
To the sons of eternal joy ;
When he took the daughter of life
Into my chambers of love,

10.

" When I found babes of bliss on my bed,
And bosoms of milk in my chambers
Filled with eternal seed,
O eternal births sung round Ahania,
In interchange sweet of their joys.

11.

" Swelled with ripeness and fat with fatness,
Bursting on winds my odours,
My ripe figs and rich pomegranates ;
In infant joy at thy feet,
O Urizen, sported and sang.

12.

" Then thou, with thy lap full of seed,
With thy hand full of generous fire,
Walked forth from the clouds of morning
On the virgins of springing joy,
On the human soul to cast
The seed of eternal science.

13.

" The sweat poured down thy temples.
To Ahania returned in evening,
The moisture awoke to birth
My mother's joys sleeping in bliss.

14.

" But now alone over rocks, mountains,
Cast out from thy lovely bosom
Cruel jealousy, selfish fear,
Self-destroying ; how can delight
Renew in the chains of darkness

Where bones of beast are strown,
On the bleak and snowy mountains
Where bones from the birth are buried
Before they see the light ? "

FROM " VALA "

THE SONG OF ENITHARMON.

I SEIZE the sphery harp, awake the strings!

At the first sound the golden sun arises from the deep
And shakes his awful hair,
The echo wakes the moon again to unbind her silver
    locks,
The golden sun bears on my song,
The nine bright spheres of harmony rise round the
    fiery king

The joy of woman in the death of her most beloved,
Who dies for love of her,
In torments of fierce jealousy and pangs of adoration.
The lover's night bears on my song,
And the nine spheres rejoice beneath my powerful
    control.

They sing unwearied to the notes of my immortal hand.
The solemn, silent moon
Reverberates the long harmony sounding upon my
    limbs.
The birds and beasts rejoice and play,
And every one seeks for his mate to prove his inmost
    joy.

Furious and terrible they sport and rend the nether deep.
The deep lifts up his rugged head,

And lost in infinite hovering wings vanishes with a cry.
The fading cry is ever dying,
The living voice is ever living in its inmost joy.

Arise, you little glancing wings, and sing your infant
    joy,
Arise and drink your bliss,
For everything that lives is holy, for the source of life
Descends to be a weeping babe.
For the earth-worm renews the moisture of the sandy
    plain.

Now my left hand I stretch abroad even to earth be-
    neath,
And strike the terrible string,
I wake sweet joys in dews of sorrow, and I plant a
    smile
In forests of affliction,
And wake the bubbling springs of life in region of dark
    death.

UNIVERSAL HUMANITY.

AND as the seed waits eagerly watching for its flower
    and fruit,
Anxious its little soul looks out into the clear expanse
To see if hungry winds are abroad with their invisible
    array ;
So Man looks out in tree, and herb, and fish, and bird,
    and beast,
Collecting up the scattered portions of his immortal
    body
Into the elemental forms of everything that grows.

He tries the sullen North wind, riding on its angry
    furrows,
The sultry South when the sun rises, and the angry
    East
When the sun sets, and the clods harden, and the
    cattle stand
Drooping, and the birds hide in their silent nests.   He
    stores his thoughts
As in store-houses in his memory.   He regulates the
    forms
Of all beneath and all above, and in the gentle West
Reposes where the sun's heat dwells.   He rises to the
    sun,
And to the planets of the night, and to the stars that
    gild
The zodiacs, and the stars that sullen stand to North
    and South,
He touches the remotest pole, and in the centre weeps
That Man should labour and sorrow, and learn and
    forget, and return
To the dark valley whence he came, and begin his
    labours anew.
In pain he sighs, in pain he labours in his universe ;
Sorrowing in birds over the deep, or howling in the wolf
Over the slain, and moaning in the cattle, and in the
    winds,
And weeping over Orc and Urizen in clouds and dis-
    mal fires,
And in cries of birth and in the groans of death his voice
Is heard throughout the universe.   Wherever a grass
    grows
Or a leaf buds the Eternal Man is seen, is heard, is felt,
And all his sorrows, till he reassumes his ancient bliss.

FROM " JERUSALEM.

From the four Prefaces to the four Chapters.

I.

To The Public.

READER—of books—of Heaven—
And of that God from whom .ˑ. . .
Who in mysterious Sinai's awful cave
To Man the wondrous art of writing gave,
Again he speaks in thunder and in fire,
Thunder of thought, and flames of fierce desire :
Even from the depths of Hell his voice I hear
Within the unfathomed caverns of my ear.
Therefore I print : nor vain my tpye shall be,—
Heaven, Earth, and Hell, henceforth shall live in har-
 mony.

   * * * *

POETRY fettered, fetters the human race. Nations are
destroyed or flourish in proportion as their poetry,
painting, and music are destroyed or flourish. The
primeval state of man was wisdom, art, and science.

II.

To The Jews.

THE fields from Islington to Marylebone,
 To Primrose Hill and Saint John's Wood,
Were builded over with pillars of gold ;
 And there Jerusalem's pillars stood.

Her little ones ran on the fields,
 The Lamb of God among them seen ;
And fair Jerusalem, His Bride,
 Among the little meadows green.

Pancras and Kentish Town repose
  Among her golden pillars high,
Among her golden arches which
  Shine upon the starry sky.

The Jews'-Harp House and the Green Man,
  The ponds where boys to bathe delight,
The fields of cows by Welling's Farm,
  Shine in Jerusalem's pleasant sight.

She walks upon our meadows green,
  The Lamb of God walks by her side,
And every English child is seen,
  Children of Jesus and His Bride.

Forgiving trespasses and sins,
  Lest Babylon, with cruel Og,
With moral and self-righteous law,
  Should crucify in Satan's synagogue.

What are those golden builders doing
  Near mournful ever-weeping Paddington—
Standing above that mighty ruin
  Where Satan the first victory won ?

Where Albion slept beneath the fatal tree ?
  And the Druid's golden knife
Rioted in human gore,
  In offerings of human life ?

They groaned aloud on London Stone,
  They groaned aloud on Tyburn's brook ;
Albion gave his deadly groan,
  And all the Atlantic mountains shook.

Albion's spectre from his loins
    Tore forth in all the pomp of war,
Satan his name : in flames of fire,
    He stretched his Druid pillars far.

Jerusalem fell from Lambeth's vale
    Down through Poplar and Old Bow.
Through Malden, and across the sea,
    In war and howling, death and woe.

The Rhine was red with human blood,
    The Danube rolled a purple tide ;
On the Euphrates Satan stood,
    And over Asia stretched his pride.

He withered up sweet Zion's hill
    From every nation of the earth ;
He withered up Jerusalem's gates,
    And in a dark land gave her birth.

He withered up the human form
    By laws of sacrifice for sin,
Till it became a mortal worm,
    But O, translucent all within !

The Divine Vision still was seen,
    Still was the human form divine ;
Weeping, in weak and mortal clay,
    O Jesus ! still the form was thine !

And thine the human face ; and thine
    The human hands, and feet, and breath
Entering through the gates of birth,
    And passing through the gates of death.

And O thou Lamb of God ! whom I
   Slew in my dark self-righteous pride,
Art thou returned to Albion's land ?
   And is Jerusalem thy Bride ?

Come to my arms, and never more
   Depart, but dwell for ever here ;
Create my spirit to thy Love,
   Subdue my spectre to thy fear.

Spectre of Albion ! warlike fiend !
   In clouds of blood and ruin rolled,
I here reclaim thee as my own,
   My selfhood ; Satan armed in gold.

Is this thy soft family love ?
   Thy cruel patriarchal pride ?
Planting thy family alone,
   Destroying all the world beside ?

A man's worst enemies are those
   Of his own house and family :
And he who makes his law a curse,
   By his own law shall surely die.

In my exchanges every land
   Shall walk ; and mine in every land,
Mutual, shall build Jerusalem,
   Both heart in heart and hand in hand.

III

TO THE DEISTS

I saw a monk of Charlemagne
Arise before my sight :
I talked with the grey monk as he stood
In the beams of infernal light.

Gibbon arose with a lash of steel,
And Voltaire with a racking wheel;
The Schools, in clouds of learning rolled.
Arose with War in iron and gold.

" Thou lazy monk ", they sound afar,
" In vain condemning glorious war ;
And in your cell you shall ever dwell.
Rise, War, and bind him in his cell."

The blood ran red from the Grey Monk's side,
His hands and feet were wounded wide ;
His body bent, his arms and knees
Like to the roots of ancient trees.

When Satan first the black bow bent,
And moral law from the Gospel rent,
He forged the law into a sword,
And spilled the blood of mercy's Lord.

Titus, Constantine, Charlemagne,
O Voltaire, Rousseau, Gibbon ; vain
Your Grecian mocks and Roman sword
Against the image of his Lord.

For a tear is an intellectual thing,
And a sigh is the sword of an angel king,
And the bitter groan of a martyr's woe
Is an arrow from the Almighty's bow.

IV

To the Christian

I give you the end of a golden string :
    Only wind it into a ball,—
It will lead you in at Heaven's gate,
    Built in Jerusalem's wall.

We are told to abstain from fleshly desires that
we may lose no time from the work of the Lord.
Every moment lost is a moment that cannot be
redeemed. Every pleasure that intermingles with
the duty of our station is a folly unredeemable, and is
planted like the seed of a wild flower among our wheat.
All the tortures of repentance are tortures of self-
reproach on account of our leaving the divine harvest
to the enemy ;—the struggles of inminglement with in-
coherent roots. I know of no other Christianity and of
no other gospel than the liberty both of body and mind to
exercise the divine arts of imagination,—imagination,
the real and eternal world of which this Vegetable
Universe is but a faint shadow, and in which we
shall live in our eternal or imaginative bodies when
these vegetable, mortal bodies are no more. The
Apostles knew of no other Gospel. What were all their
spiritual gifts ? What is the Divine Spirit ? Is the Holy
Ghost any other than an intellectual fountain ? What
is the harvest of the Gospel, and its labours ? What
is that talent which it is a curse to hide ? What are the
treasures of Heaven which we are to lay up for ourselves ?
Are they any other than mental studies and perfor-
mances ? What are all the gifts of the Gospel ? Are
they not all mental gifts ? Is God a spirit who must
be worshipped in spirit and in truth ? And are not
the gifts of the Spirit everything to man ? O ye
religious, discountenance every one among you who
shall pretend to despise art and science. I call upon
you in the name of Jesus ! What is the life of man
but art and science ? Is it meat and drink ? Is not
the body more than raiment ? What is mortality
but the things relating to the body which dies ? What

is immortality but the things relating to the spirit which lives eternally ? What is the joy of Heaven but improvement in the things of the spirit ? What are the pains of Hell but ignorance, idleness, bodily lust, and the devastation of the things of the spirit ? Answer this for yourselves, and expel from among you those who pretend to despise the labours of art and science which alone are the labours of the Gospel. Is not this plain and manifest to the thought ? Can you think at all and not pronounce heartily that to labour in knowledge is to build up Jerusalem, and to despise knowledge is to despise Jerusalem and her builders ? And remember, he who despises and mocks a mental gift in another, calling it pride, and selfishness, and sin, mocks Jesus, the giver of every mental gift, which always appear to the ignorance-loving hypocrite as sins. But that which is a sin in the sight of cruel man is not so in the sight of our kind God. Let every Christian as much as in him lies, engage himself openly and publicly before all the world in some mental pursuit for the building of Jerusalem.

I stood among my valleys of the South,
And saw a flame of fire, even as a wheel
Of fire surrounding all the heavens : it went
From West to East against the current of
Creation, and devoured all things in its loud
Fury and thundering course round heaven and earth.
By it the sun was rolled into an orb ;
By it the moon faded into a globe
Travelling through the night ; for, from its dire
And restless fury Man himself shrunk up
Into a little root a fathom long,

And I asked a watcher and holy-one
Its name He answered: " It is the wheel of religion. "
I wept and said : " Is this the law of Jesus,—
This terrible devouring sword turning every way ? "
He answered : " Jesus died because He strove
Against the current of this wheel : its name
Is Caiaphas, the dark preacher of Death,

Of sin, of sorrow, and of punishment ;
Opposing nature : It is natural religion.
But Jesus is the bright preacher of Life,
Creating nature from this fiery law,
By self-denial and forgiveness of sin.
Go therefore, cast out devils in Christ's name,
Heal thou the sick of spiritual disease,
Pity the evil : for thou art not sent
To smite with terror and with punishments
Those that are sick, like to the Pharisees
Crucifying and encompassing sea and land
For proselytes to tyranny and wrath.
But to the publicans and harlots go :
Teach them true happiness, but let no curse
Go forth out of thy mouth to blight their peace :
For Hell is opened to Heaven : thine eyes behold
The dungeons burst, and the prisoners set free."

> England ! awake ! awake ! awake !
>   Jerusalem thy sister calls !
> Why wilt thou sleep the sleep of death,
>   And close her from thy ancient walls?
>
> Thy hills and valleys felt her feet
>   Gently upon their bosoms move :
> Thy gates beheld sweet Zion's ways ;
>   Then was a time of joy and love.

And now the time returns again :
  Our souls exult : and London's towers
Receive the Lamb of God to dwell
  In England's green and pleasant bowers.

FROM THE POEM ITSELF

BROTHERHOOD AND RESTRICTION

In Great Eternity every particular form gives forth or
    emanates
Its own peculiar light, and the form is the Divine Vision,
And the light is His garment. This is Jerusalem in
    every man,
A tent and tabernacle of mutual forgiveness, male
    and female clothings.
And Jerusalem is called Liberty among the children
    of Albion.

THE VEIL OF NATURE

Why should punishment weave the veil with iron
    wheels of war,
When forgiveness might weave it with wings of cheru-
    bim ?

LOVE AND ITS NEGATIONS

They know not why they love, nor wherefore they
    sicken and die,
Calling that holy love which is envy, revenge, and
    cruelty,
Which separated the stars from the mountains, the
    mountains from man,
And left man a little grovelling root outside of him-
    self.

VENGEANCE

What shall I do ? What could I do if I could find
  these criminals ?
I could not dare to take vengeance, for all things are
  so constructed
And builded by the Divine Hand that the sinner
  shall always escape ;
And he who takes vengeance is alone the criminal of
  Providence.
If I should dare to lift my finger on a grain of sand,
In way of vengeance, I punish the already punished.
  Of whom
Should I pity if I pity not the sinner who is gone
  astray ?
O Albion, if thou takest vengeance, if thou revengest
  thy wrongs,
Thou art for ever lost.   What can I do to hinder the
  sons
Of Albion from taking vengeance, or how shall I them
  persuade ?

TRUTH AND FALSEHOOD

I labour day and night : I behold the soft affections
Condense beneath my hammer into forms of cruelty,
But still I labour in hope, though still my tears flow
  down,
That he who will not defend Truth may be compelled
  to defend
A Lie, that he may be snared and caught, and snared
  and taken,
That enthusiasm and life may not cease.

CREATION

I must create a system, or be enslaved by another
   man's.
I will not reason compare.   My business is to create.

REASON

And this is the manner of the sons of Albion in their
   strength :
They take the two contraries which are called qualities,
   with which
Every substance is clothed.   They name them good
   and evil.
From them they make an abstract, which is a negation
Not only of the substance from which it is derived,
A murderer of its own body, but also a murderer
Of every Divine Member.   It is the reasoning power,
An abstract objecting power that negatives every-
   thing.
This is the spectre of man, the holy reasoning power,
And in its holiness is closed the Abomination of Deso-
   lation.

ANALYSIS

Why wilt thou number every little fibre of my soul,
Spreading them out before the sun like stalks of flax
   to dry ?
The infant joy is beautiful, but its anatomy
Horrible, ghast, and deadly.   Nought shalt thou
   find in it
But dark despair and everlasting brooding melancholy.

SEXUAL LOVE

O that I could abstain from wrath! O that the
    Lamb
Of God would look upon me and pity me in my fury.
In anguish of regeneration, in terrors of self-annihi-
    lation,
Pity must join together what wrath has torn in sunder,
And the religion of generation which was meant for
    the destruction
Of Jerusalem become her covering till the time of
    the end.
O holy generation, image of regeneration!
O point of mutual forgiveness between enemies!
Birthplace of the Lamb of God, incomprehensible,
The dead despise thee, and scorn thee, and cast thee
    out as accursed,
Seeing the Lamb of God in thy gardens and palaces.

THE DEATH OF CHRIST

Jesus said, " Would'st thou love one who had never
    died
For thee, or ever die for one who had not died for
    thee?
And if God dieth not for man, and giveth not Himself
Eternally for man, man could not exist, for man is
    love,
As God is love.   Every kindness to another is a little
    Death
In the Divine Image, nor can man exist but by brother-
    hood.

FROM " MILTON "

AND did those feet in ancient time
  Walk upon England's mountain green ?
And was the holy Lamb of God
  On England's pleasant pastures seen ?

And did the Countenance Divine
  Shine forth upon our clouded hills ?
And was Jerusalem builded here
  Among these dark Satanic mills ?

Bring me my bow of burning gold !
  Bring me my arrows of desire !
Bring me my spear : O clouds, unfold !
  Bring me my chariot of fire !

I will not cease from mental fight,
  Nor shall my sword sleep in my hand,
Till we have built Jerusalem
  In England's green and pleasant land.

THE FLAT WORLD OF IMAGINATION

The sky is an immortal tent built by the sons of Los,
And every space that a man views around his dwelling-
    place,
Standing on his own roof, or in his garden on a mount
Of twenty-five cubits in height, such space is his
    universe,
And on its verse the sun rises and sets, the clouds
    bow
To meet the flat earth and the sea in such an ordered
    space :

The starry heavens reach no farther, but here bend
    and set
On all sides, and the two poles turn on their valves
    of gold ;
And if he move his dwelling-place, his heavens also
    move
Where'er he goes, and all his neighbourhood bewails
    his loss.
Such are the spaces called earth, and such its dimen-
    sion.
As to that false appearance which appears to the
    reasoner
As of a globe rolling through voidness, it is a delusion
    of Ulro.

TIME

Every time less than a pulsation of the artery
Is equal in its period and value to six thousand years.
For in this period the poet's work is done, and all the
    great
Events of time start forth and are conceived in such
    a period,
Within a moment : a pulsation of the artery.

SPACE

Every space larger than a red globule of man's blood
Is visionary, and is created by the hammer of Los.
And every space smaller than a globule of man's
    blood opens
Into eternity, of which the vegetable earth is but a
    shadow.

THE MORNING SONG OF THE BIRDS

THE lark sitting upon his earthy bed, just as the morn
Appears, listens silent, then springing from the waving
    cornfield,
Loud he leads the choir of Day : thrill ! thrill ! thrill !
Mounting upon the wings of light into the great ex-
    panse,
Reaching against the lovely blue and shining heavenly
    skies ;
His little throat labours with inspiration ; every
    feather
On throat and breast and wings vibrates with the
    effluence divine,
All Nature listens silent to him, and the awful sun
Stands still upon the mountain looking on the little
    bird
With eyes of soft humility, and wonder, love, and
    awe.
Then loud from their green covert all the birds begin
    their song :
The thrush, the linnet, and the goldfinch, robin, and
    the wren,
Awake the sun from his sweet reverie on the mountain.

THE MORNING SCENT OF THE FLOWERS

THOU perceivest the flowers put forth their precious
    odours,
And none can tell how from so small a centre come
    such sweets,
Forgetting that within that centre Eternity expands
Its everduring doors, that Og and Anak fiercely guard.

First ere the morning breaks, joy opens in the flowery
    bosoms,
Joy even to tears, which the sun rising dries : first
    the wild thyme,
And meadowsweet, downy, and soft waving among
    the reeds,
Light springing on the air lead the sweet dance ; they
    wake
The honeysuckle sleeping on the oak, the flaunting
    beauty
Revels along upon the wind ; the white-thorn lovely
    May
Opens her many lovely eyes ; listening the rose still
    sleeps,
None dare to wake her ; soon she bursts her crimson-
    curtained bed,
And comes forth in the majesty of beauty. Every
    flower,
The pink, the jessamine, the wallflower and the carna-
    tion,
The jonquil ; the mild lily opens her heavens ; every
    tree
And flower and herb soon fill the air with an innumera-
    ble dance,
Yet all in order, sweet and lovely. Men are sick with
    Love.

PROSE FRAGMENTS.

PROSE FRAGMENTS.

ON HIS PICTURE OF THE CANTERBURY
PILGRIMS.

THE time chosen is early morning before sunrise, when the jolly company are leaving the Tabarde Inn. The Knight and Squire with the Squire's yeoman lead the Procession; next follow the youthful Abbess, her nun, and three priests; —her greyhounds attend her—

> " Of small hounds had she, that she feed
> With roast flesh, milk, and wastel bread."

Next follow the Friar and Monk, and then the Tapiser, the Pardoner, and the Sompnour and Manciple. After this " Our Host," who occupies the centre of the cavalcade, and directs them to the Knight, as the person who would be likely to commence their task of each telling a tale in their order. After the Host follows the Shipman, the Haberdasher, the Dyer, the Franklin, the Physician, the Ploughman, the Lawyer, the Poor Parson, the Merchant, the Wife of Bath, the Miller, the Cook, the Oxford Scholar, Chaucer himself; and the Reeve comes as Chaucer has described :—

> " And ever he rode hindermost of the rout."

These last are issuing from the gateway of the Inn; the Cook and the Wife of Bath are both taking their morning's draught of comfort. Spectators stand at the gateway of the Inn, and are composed of an old Man, a Woman, and a Child.

The Landscape is an eastward view of the country from the Tabarde Inn, in Southwark, as it may be supposed to have appeared in Chaucer's time; interspersed with cottages and villages. The first beams of the sun are seen above the horizon; some buildings and spires indicate the position of the Great City. The Inn is a Gothic building which Thynne in his Glossary says was the lodging of the Abbot of Hyde by Winchester. On the Inn is inscribed its title, and a proper advantage is taken of this circumstance to describe the subject of the picture. The words written over the gateway of the Inn are as follows :—

" The Tabarde Inn, by Henry Baillie, the lodgynge house for Pilgrims who journey to St. Thomas' Shrine at Canterbury."

The characters of Chaucer's Pilgrims are the characters which compose all ages and nations. As one age falls another rises different to mortal sight, but to immortals only the same; for we see the same characters repeated again and again, in animals, vegetables, minerals, and in men. Nothing new occurs in identical existence; accident ever varies. Substance can never suffer change or decay.

Of Chaucer's characters as described in His Canterbury Tales some of the names or titles are altered by time, but the characters themselves ever remain unaltered; and consequently they are the physiognomies or lineaments of universal human life beyond which Nature never steps. Names alter; things never alter. I have known multitudes of those who would have been monks in the age of monkery, and who in this deistical age are deists. As Newton numbered the stars and as Linneus has numbered the plants, so Chaucer numbered the classes of men.

The painter has consequently varied the heads and forms of his personages into all Nature's varieties. The horses he has also varied to accord to their riders; the costume is correct according to authentic monuments.

The Knight and the Squire and the Squire's Yeoman lead the procession, as Chaucer has also placed them first in his prologue. The Knight is a true hero, a good, great, and wise man; his whole-length portrait on horseback as written by Chaucer cannot be surpassed. He has spent life in the field, has ever been a conqueror, and is that species of character which in every age stands as the guardian of man against the oppressor. His son is like him, with the germ of perhaps greater perfection still, as he blends literature and the arts with his warlike studies. Their dress and their horses are of the first rate, without ostentation, and with all the true grandeur that unaffected simplicity when in high rank always displays. The Squire's Yeoman is also a great character, a man perfectly knowing in his profession :

" And in his hand he bore a mighty bow."

Chaucer describes here a mighty man ; one who, in war, is the worthy attendant on noble heroes.

The Prioress follows these with her female chaplain.

" Another Nonne also with her had she,
That was her Chapelaine, and Priestes three."

This Lady is described also as of the first rank, rich and honoured. She has certain peculiarities and little delicate affectations, not unbecoming in her, being accompanied with what is truly grand and really polite ; her person and face Chaucer has described with minuteness ; it is very elegant, and was the beauty of our ancestors until after Elizabeth's time, when voluptuousness and folly began to be accounted beautiful.

Her companion and her three priests were no doubt all perfectly delineated in those parts of Chaucer's work which are now lost ; we ought to suppose them suitable attendants on rank and fashion.

The Monk follows these with the Friar. The painter has also grouped with these the Pardoner and the Sompnour and the Manciple, and has here also introduced one of the rich citizens of London ; characters likely to ride in company, all being above the common rank of life, or attendants on those who were so.

For the Monk is described by Chaucer as a man of the first rank in society, noble, rich, and expensively attended ; he is a leader of the age, with certain humorous accompaniments in his character that do not degrade, but render him an object of dignified mirth,—but also with other accompaniments not so respectable.

The Friar is a character of a mixed kind :

> " A Friar there was, a wanton and a merry ; "

but in his office he is said to be a " full solemn man ; " eloquent,
amorous, witty, and satirical ; young, handsome, and rich ;
he is a complete rogue, with constitutional gaiety enough to
make him a master of all the pleasures in the world.

> " His neck white as the flour de lis,
>   Thereto was he strong as a champi oun."

It is necessary here to speak of Chaucer's own character
that I may set certain mistaken critics right in their conception
of the humour and fun that occur on the journey. Chaucer
himself is the great poetic observer of men who in every age is
born to record and eternize its acts.   This he does as a master,
as a father, and superior, who looks down on their little fol-
lies, from the Emperor to the Miller, sometimes with severity,
oftener with joke and sport.

Accordingly Chaucer has made his Monk a great tragedian,
one who studied poetical art.   So much so that the generous
Knight is, in the compassionate dictates of his soul, compelled
to cry out :

> " ' Ho,' quoth the Knyght,—' good sir, no more of this ;
>   That ye have said is right ynough I wis,
>   And mokell more ; for little heaviness
>   Is right ynough for much folk, as I guesse.
>   I say, for me, it is a great disease.
>   Whereas men have been in wealth and ease
>   To heare of their sudden fall,—alas !
>   And the contrary is joy, and solas.' "

The Monk's definition of tragedy in the proem to his tale
is worth repeating :

> " Tragedie is to tell a certain story,
>   As old books us maken memory,
>   Of hem that stood in great prosperity,
>   And (who) be fallen out of high degree
>   To miserie, and ended wretchedly."

Though a man of luxury, pride, and pleasure, he is a master
of art and learning, though affecting to despise it.   Those,
who think that the proud Huntsman and noble Housekeeper

Chaucer's Monk is intended for a buffoon or a burlesque character, know little of Chaucer.

For the Host who follows this group, and holds the centre of the cavalcade, is a first-rate character, and his jokes are no trifles; they are always,—though uttered with audacity equally free with the Lord and the Peasant,—they are always substantially and weightily expressive of knowledge and experience; Henry Baillie, the keeper of the greatest Inn of the greatest City, for such was the Tabarde Inn in Southwark near London,—our Host was also a leader of the age.

By way of illustration, I instance Shakespeare's Witches in "Macbeth." Those who dress them for the stage consider them as wretched old women, and not, as Shakespeare intended, the Goddesses of Destiny. This shows how Chaucer has been misunderstood in his sublime work. Shakespeare's Fairies, also, are the rulers of the vegetable world, and so are Chaucer's. Let them be so understood, and then the poet will be understood, and not else.

But I have omitted to speak of a very prominent character, the Pardoner, the Age's Knave, who always commands and domineers over the high and low vulgar. This man is sent in every age for a rod and scourge, and for a blight, for a trial of men, to divide the classes of men. He is in the most holy sanctuary, and he is suffered by Providence, for wise ends, and has also his great use and his grand leading destiny.

His companion, the Sompnour, is also a Devil of the first magnitude, grand, terrific, rich; and honoured in the rank of which he holds the destiny. The uses to Society are perhaps equal of the Devil and the Angel. Their sublimity, who can dispute?

> " In danger had he at his own gise,
> The young girls of his diocese,
> And he knew well their counsel," etc.

The principal figure in the next group is the Good Parson; an Apostle, a real Messenger of Heaven, sent in every age for its light and its warmth. The man is beloved and venerated by all, and neglected by all. He serves all, and is served by none. He is, according to a Christ's definition, the greatest of his age, yet he is a Poor Parson of a town. Read Chaucer's description of the Good Parson, and bow the head and knee to Him, Who in every age sends us such a burning and a shining light. Search, O ye rich and powerful, for these men, and obey their counsel ; then shall the golden age return. But alas ! you will not easily distinguish him from the Friar or the Pardoner. They, also, are " full solemn men," and *their* counsel you will continue to follow.

I have placed by his side the Sergeant at Lawe, who appears delighted to ride in his company, and between him and his brother the Ploughman, as I wish men of law would always ride with them, and take their counsel, especially in all difficult points. Chaucer's Lawyer is a character of great venerableness, a Judge, a real master of the jurisprudence of his age.

The Doctor of Physic is in this group, and the Franklin, the voluptuous country gentleman, contrasted with the Physician, and on his other hand, with two citizens of London. Chaucer's characters live age after age. Every age is a Canterbury Pilgrimage. We all pass on, each sustaining one or other of these characters ; nor can a child be born who is not one or other of these characters of Chaucer. The Doctor of Physic is described as the first of his profession ; perfect, learned, completely Master and Doctor in his art. Thus the reader will observe that Chaucer makes every one of his characters perfect in his kind. Every one is an Antique Statue, the image of a class, not of an imperfect individual.

This group also would furnish substantial matter on which volumes might be written. The Franklin is one who keeps open table, who is the genius of eating and drinking, like Bacchus. As the Doctor of Physic is the Æsculapius, the Host is the Silenus, the Squire is the Apollo, the Miller is the Hercules, etc. Chaucer's characters are a description of the eternal principles that exist in all ages. The Franklin is voluptuousness itself, most nobly portrayed.—

" It snewed in his house of meat and drink."

The Ploughman is simplicity itself, with wisdom and strength for its stamina. Chaucer has divided the ancient character of Hercules between his Miller and his Ploughman. Benevolence is the Ploughman's great characteristic. He is thin with excessive labour, and not with old age, as some have supposed :

> " He would threash, and thereto dike and delve,
> For Christe's sake, for every poure wight,
> Withouten hire, if it lay in his might."

Visions of these eternal principles or characters of human life appear to poets in all ages. The Grebian gods were the ancient Cherubim of Phœnicia, but the Greeks, and since them, the Moderns, have neglected to subdue the gods of Priam. These gods are visions of the eternal attributes or divine names, which, when erected into gods, become destructive to humanity. Thought to be the servants and not the masters of man or of society. They ought to be made to sacrifice to man, and not man compelled to sacrifice to them ; for when separated from man, or humanity, who is Jesus, the Saviour, the vine of eternity, they are thieves and rebels ; they are destroyers.

The Ploughman of Chaucer is Hercules in his supreme eternal state, divided from his spectrous shadow, which is the Miller, a terrible fellow, such as exists in all times and places for the trial of men, to astonish every neighbourhood with brutal strength and courage, to get rich and powerful, to curb the pride of man.

The Reeve and the Manciple are two characters of consummate worldly wisdom. The Shipman, or Sailor, is a similar genius of Ulyssian art, but with the highest courage superadded.

The Citizens and their Cook are each leaders of a class. Chaucer has been somehow made to number four Citizens, which would make his whole company, himself included, thirty-one. But he says there were but nine-and-twenty in his company—

> " Full nine-and-twenty in a company."

The Webbe, or Weaver, and the Tapiser, or Tapestry Weaver, appear to me to be the same person, but this is only an opinion, for full " nine-and-twenty " may singify one more or less. But I dare say that Chaucer wrote, " A Webbe Dyer," that is a cloth dyer—

> " A Webbe Dyer, and a Tapiser."

The Merchant cannot be one of the three Citizens, as his dress is different and his character is more marked, whereas Chaucer says of his rich Citizen—

> " All were y-clothed in o liverie."

The characters of women Chaucer has divided into two classes, the Lady Prioress and the Wife of Bath. Are not these leaders of the ages of men? The Lady Prioress in some ages predominates, and in some the Wife of Bath, in whose character Chaucer has been equally minute and exact, because she is also a scourge and a blight. I shall say no more of her, nor expose what Chaucer has left hidden. Let the young reader study what he has said of her. It is useful as a scarecrow. There are such characters born—too many for the peace of the world.

I come at length to the Clerk of Oxenford. This character varies from that of Chaucer as the contemplative philosopher varies from the poetical genius. There are always these two classes of learned sages the poetical and the philosophical. The painter has put them side by side, as if the youthful Clerk had put himself under the tuition of the mature poet. Let the philosopher always be the servant and scholar of inspiration, and all will be happy.

Such are the characters that compose this picture, which was painted in self-defence against the insolent and envious imputation of unfitness for finished and scientific art,—and this imputation most artfully and industriously endeavoured to be propagated among the public by ignorant hirelings. The painter courts comparison with his competitors, who, having received fourteen hundred guineas and more from the profits of *his* designs in that well-known work, Designs for Blair's Grave, have left him to shift for himself, while others, more obedient to an employer's opinions and directions, are employed at great expense to produce works in succession to his, by which they acquired public patronage. This has hitherto been his lot, to get patronage for others and then to be left and neglected, and his work, which gained that patronage, cried down as eccentricity and madness—as unfinished and neglected by the artist's violent temper. He is sure the works now exhibited will give the lie to such aspersions.

Those who say that men are led by interest are knaves. A knavish character will often say, " Of what interest is it to me to do—so and so ? " I answer, " Of none at all, but the contrary, as you well know. It is of malice and envy that you have done this therefore I am aware of you, because I know that you act, not from interest, but from malice, even to your own destruction." It is therefore become a duty which Mr. B. owes to the Public, who have always recognized him, and patronized him, however hidden by artifices, that he should not suffer such things to be done, or be hindered from the public exhibition of his finished production by any calumnies in future.

The character and expression in this picture could never have been produced with Rubens' light and shadow, or with Rembrandt's or anything Venetian or Flemish. The Venetian and Flemish practice is broken lines, broken masses, and broken colours. Mr. B.'s practice is unbroken lines, unbroken masses, and unbroken colours. Their art is to lose form. His art is to find form and keep it. His arts are opposite to theirs in all things.

As there is a class of men whose sole delight is in the destruction of men, so there is a class of artists whose whole art and science is frabricated for this purpose of destroying art. Who these are is soon known. " By their works ye shall know them." All who endeavour to raise up a style against Raphael, Michael Angelo, and the Antique, those who separate Painting from Drawing, who look if a picture is well drawn, and, if it is, immediately cry out that it cannot be well coloured—those are the men.

But to show the stupidity of this class of men, nothing need be done but to examine my rival's prospectus.

The five first characters in Chaucer, the Knight and the Squire he has put among his rabble, and indeed his prospectus calls the Squire the " fop of Chaucer's age." Now hear Chaucer :

> " Of his stature he was of even length,
> And wonderly deliver, and of great strength.
> And he had been some time in Chivauchy.
> In Flanders, in Artois, and in Picardy,
> And borne him well, as of so litele space."

Was this a fop ?

> " Well could he sit a horse, and faire ride
> He could songs make, eke well indite,
> Joust, and eke dance, portray, and well write."

Was this a fop ?

" Curteis he was, and meek and serviceable,
    And kerft before his fader at the table."

Was this a fop ?

It is the same with all his characters. He had done all by chance, or perhaps his fortune—money, money ! According to his prospectus he has three Monks. These he cannot find in Chaucer, who has only one Monk, and that, no vulgar character, as he has endeavoured to make him. When men cannot read they should not pretend to paint. To be sure, Chaucer is a little difficult to him who has only blundered over novels and catch-penny trifles of booksellers, yet a little pains ought to be taken even by the ignorant and weak. He has put the Reeve, a vulgar fellow, between his Knight and Squire, as if he was resolved to go contrary to everything in Chaucer, who says of the Reeve :

" And ever he rode hindermost of the rout."

In this manner he has jumbled his dumb dollies together, and is praised by his equals for it, for both himself and his friend are equally masters of Chaucer's language. They both think that the Wife of Bath is a young, beautiful, blooming damsel, and H—— says, that she is the " Fair Wife of Bath ", and that " the Spring appears in her cheeks." Now hear what Chaucer has made her say of herself—who is no modest one :

" But Lord when it remembreth me
    Upon my youth and on my joleity,
    It tickleth me about the hearte-root,
    Unto this day it doth my hearte boot
    That I have had my world as in my time,
    But age, alas, that all will envenime,
    Hath me bereft my beauty and my pith.
    Let go ! Farewell ! The Devil go therewith,
    The flour is gone ; there is no more to tell,
    The bran, as best I can, I now mote sell.
    And yet to be right merry I will fond
    Now forth, to tell about my fourth husband."

She has had four husbands ; a fit subject for this painter.

Yet the painter ought to be very much offended with his friend H——, who has called his "a common scene", and "very ordinary forms", which is the truest part of all, for it is so, and very wretchedly so indeed. What merit can there be in a picture of which such words are spoken with truth ?

But the prospectus says that the painter has represented Chaucer himself as a knave who thrusts himself among honest people to make game of and laugh at them ; though I must do justice to the painter and say that he has made him look more like a fool than a knave. But it appears in all the writings of Chaucer and particularly in his Canterbury Tales, that he was very devout, and paid respect to true enthusiastic superstition. He has laughed at his knaves and fools, as I do now, but he has respected his True Pilgrims, who are a majority of his company, and are not thrown together in the random manner that Mr. S—— has done. Chaucer has nowhere called the Ploughman old, worn out with "age and labour," as the prospectus has represented him, and says that the picture has done so too. He is worn down with labour, but not with age. How spots of brown and yellow smeared about at random can be either young or old I cannot see. It may be an old man ; it may be a young man ; it may be anything that a prospectus pleases. But I know that where there are no lineaments there can be no character. And what connoisseurs call touch, I know by experience must be the destruction of all character and expression as it is of every lineament.

The scene of Mr. S——'s picture is by Dulwich Hills, which was not the way to Canterbury, but perhaps the painter thought he would give them a ride round about because they were a burlesque set of scarecrows not worth any man's respect or care.

But the painter's thought being always upon gold, he has introduced a character that Chaucer has not, namely, a Goldsmith, for so the prospectus tells us. Why he introduced a Goldsmith, and what is the wit, the prospectus does not explain. But it takes care to mention the reserve and modesty of the painter. This makes a good epigram enough :

> " The fox, the mole, the beetle, and the bat
> By sweet reserve and modesty get fat."

But the prospectus tells us that the painter has introduced a
" Sea-Captain." Chaucer has a Ship-man, a Sailor, a trading
Master of a vessel, called by courtesy Captain, as every master
of a boat is ; but this does not make him a Sea-Captain. Chau-
cer has purposely omitted such a personage, as it only exists in
certain periods: it is the soldier by sea. He who would be a
soldier in inland nations is a sea-captain in commercial nations·

All is misconceived, and its mis-execution is equal to its
misconception. I have no objection to Rubens and Rembrandt
being employed, or even to their living in a palace. But it
shall not be at the expense of Raphael and Michael Angelo
living in a cottage, and in contempt and derision. I have been
scorned long enough by these fellows, who owe me all that they
have. It shall be so no longer.

> " I found them blind : I taught them how to see ;
> And now they know neither themselves nor me."

IDENTITY.

IN eternity one thing never changes into another thing. Each
identity is eternal. Consequently Apuleius' Golden Ass and
Ovid's Metamorphoses and others of the like kind are fable ;
yet they contain vision in a sublime degree, being derived from
real vision in more ancient writings. Lot's wife being changed
into a pillar of salt alludes to the mortal body being made a
permanent statue but not changed or transformed into another
identity, while it retains its own individuality. A man can
never become ass or horse. Some are born with shapes of men
who are both. But eternal identity is one thing, and corporeal
vegetation is another thing. Changing water into wine by
Jesus and into blood by Moses relates to vegetable nature also.

The nature of visionary fancy or imagination is very little
known and the eternal nature and permanence of its ever-
existent images is considered less permanent than the things
of vegetable and generative nature. Yet the oak dies as well
as the lettuce, but its eternal image or individuality never dies,
but renews by its seed. Just so the imaginative image returns
by the seed of contemplative thought. The writings of the
Prophets illustrate these conceptions of the visionary fancy, by
their various sublime and divine images as seen in the world of
vision.

The world of imagination is the world of eternity. It is the divine bosom into which we shall all go after the death of the vegetated body. The world of imagination is infinite and eternal, whereas the world of generation or vegetation is finite and temporal. There exist in that eternal world the eternal realities of everything which we see reflected in this vegetable glass of nature.

All things are comprehended in their eternal forms in the divine body of the Saviour, the true vine of eternity, the human imagination, Who apppeared to me as coming to judgment among His saints, and throwing off the temporal that the eternal might be established. Around Him are seen the images of existence according to a certain order suited to my imaginative energy.

Minute Knowledge.

If the spectator could enter into these images in his imagination, approaching them on the fiery chariot of his contemplative thought,—if he could enter into Noah's rainbow, could make a friend and companion of one of these images of wonder, which always entreat him to leave mortal things (as he must know), then would he arise from the grave, then would he meet the Lord in the air, and then he would be happy. General knowledge is remote knowledge. It is in particulars that wisdom consists and happiness too. Both in art and in life general masses are as much art as a pasteboard man is human. Every man has eyes, nose, and mouth. This every idiot knows. But he who enters into and discriminates most minutely the manners and intentions, the characters in all their branches, is the alone wise or sensible man, and on this discrimination all art is founded. I entreat, then, that the spectator will attend to the hands and feet, to the lineaments of the countenance. They are all descriptive of character, and not a line is drawn without intention, and that most discriminate and particular. As poetry admits not a letter that is insignificant, so painting admits not a grain of sand or a blade of grass insignificant—much less an insignificant blur or mark.

The Nature of a Last Judgment.

A last Judgment is necessary because fools flourish. Nations flourish under wise rulers and are depressed under foolish rulers. It is the same with individuals as with nations. Works of art can only be produced in perfection where the man is either in affluence or above the care of it. Poverty is the fool's rod which at last is turned on his own back. That is a Last Judgment when men of real art govern and pretenders fall. Some people, and not a few artists, have asserted that the painter of this people would not have done so well if he had been properly encouraged. Let those who think so reflect on the state of nations under poverty and their incapability of art. Though art is above either, the argument is better for affluence than poverty, and though he would not have been a greater artist, he would have produced greater works of art in proportion to his means. A Last Judgment is not for the purpose of making bad men better but of hindering them from oppressing the good.

All life consists of these two, throwing off error and knaves from our company continually, and receiving truth, or wise men, into our company continually. He who is out of the church and opposes it is no less an agent of religion than he who is in it. No man can embrace true art until he has explored and cast out false art, such is the nature of mortal things, or he will be himself cast out by those who have already embraced true art. Thus my picture is a history of art and science, the foundation of society, which is humanity itself. What are the gifts of the spirit but mental gifts? When any individual rejects error and embraces truth, a Last Judgment passes upon that individual.

Why Men enter Heaven.

MEN are admitted into heaven not because they have curbed and governed their passions, or have no passions, but because they have cultivated their understandings. The treasures of heaven are not negations of passion, but realities of intellect, from which the passions emanate, uncurbed in their eternal glory. The fool shall not enter into heaven, let him be ever so holy. Holiness is not the price of entrance into heaven. Those who are cast out are all those who, having no passions of their own, because no intellect, have spent their lives in curbing and governing other people's by the various arts of poverty and cruelty of all kinds. The modern church crucifies Christ with the head downwards. Woe, woe, woe to you hypocrites!

Learning without Imagination.

This subject—an experiment picture—is taken from the visions of Emanuel Swedenborg. The learned who strive to ascend into heaven by means of learning appear to children like dead horses when repelled by the celestial spheres. The works of this visionary are well worthy the attention of painters and poets; they are foundations for grand things. The reason they have not been more attended to is, because corporeal demons have gained a predominance. Who the leaders of these are will be shown below. Unworthy men, who gain fame among men, continue to govern mankind after death, and in their spiritual bodies oppose the spirits of those who worthily are famous, and as Swedenborg observes, shut the doors of mind and of thought by placing learning above inspiration.

Form and Substance are One.

No man can improve an original invention; nor can an original invention exist without execution organized, delineated, and articulated, either by God or man. I do not mean smoothed up, and niggled, and poco-pen'd, and all the beauties paled out, blurred, and blotted, but drawn with a firm and. decided hand at once, like Michael Angelo, Shakespeare, and Milton. I have heard many people say, "Give me the ideas, it is not matter what words you put them into", and others say, " Give me the design, it is no matter for the execution." These people knew enough of artifice, but nothing of art. Ideas cannot be given but in their minutely appropriate words, nor can a design be made without its minutely appropriate execution.

Good and Evil.

Many persons, such as Paine and Voltaire, with some of the ancient Greeks, say—" We will not converse concerning good and evil : we will live in paradise and liberty." You may do so in spirit, but not in the mortal body as you pretend, until after a Last Judgment. For in paradise they have no corporeal and mortal body. *That* originated with the fall and was called Death, and cannot be removed but by a Last Judgment. While we are in the world of mortality we must suffer. The whole Creation groans to be delivered.

The Clearness of Vision.

THE Prophets describe what they saw in vision as real and existing men, whom they saw with their imaginative and immortal organs; the Apostles the same; the clearer the organ the more distinct the object. A spirit and a vision are not, as the modern philosophy supposes, a cloudy vapour, or a nothing; they are organized and minutely articulated beyond all that the mortal and perishing nature can produce. He who does not imagine in stronger and better lineaments, and in stronger and better light, than his perishing mortal eye can see, does not imagine at all. The painter of this work asserts that all his imaginations appear to him infinitely more perfect and more minutely organized than anything seen by his mortal eye. Spirits are organized men.

Outline in Art and Life.

THE great and golden rule of art, as well as of life, is this:—That the more distinct, sharp, and wiry the bounding line, the more perfect the work of art : and the less keen and sharp, the greater is the evidence of weak imitation, plagiarism and bungling. Great inventors in all ages knew this. Protogenes and Apelles knew each other by this line. Raphael, and Michael Angelo, and Albert Durer are known by this, and this alone. The want of this determinate and bounding form evidences the idea of want in the artist's mind, and the pretence of plagiary in all its branches. How do we distinguish the oak from the beech, the horse from the ox, but by the bounding outline? How do we distinguish one face or countenance from another, but by the bounding line and its infinite inflections and movements? What is it that builds a house and plants a garden but the definite and determinate? What is it that distinguishes honesty from knavery but the hard and wiry line of rectitude and certainty in the actions and intentions? Leave out this line, and you leave out life itself; all is chaos again, and the line of the Almighty must be drawn out upon it before man or beast can exist.

THE TREES OF KNOWLEDGE AND OF LIFE.

THE combats of good and evil is eating of the Tree of Know-
ledge. The combats of truth and error is eating of the Tree
of Life. These are universal and particular. Each are per-
sonified. There is not an error but has a man for its agent;
that is, it is a man. There is not a truth but it has also a
man. Good and evil are qualities in every man whether a
good or evil man. These are enemies, and destroy one another
by every means in their power, whether of deceit or open
violence. The Deist and the Christian are but the results
of these opposing Natures. Many are Deists who, under
certain circumstances, would have been Christians in outward
appearance ; Voltaire was one of this number. He was as
intolerant as an inquisitor. Manners make the man, not
habits. It is the same in heart. " By their fruits ye shall
know them." The knave who is converted to Deism, and the
knave who is converted to Christianity is still a knave. But
he himself will not know it, though everybody else does. Christ
comes, as He came at first, to deliver those who are bound
under the knave, not to deliver the knave. He comes to
deliver Man the Accused not Satan the Accuser. We do
not find anywhere that Satan is accused of sin. He is only
accused of unbelief, and thereby of drawing man into sin that
he may accuse him. Such is the last Judgment ; a deliver-
ance from Satan's accusation. Satan thinks that sin is dis-
pleasing to God. He ought to know that nothing is displeasing
to God but unbelief, and eating of the tree of knowledge of good
and evil.

THERE IS NO NATURAL RELIGION.—I.

THE VOICE OF ONE CRYING IN THE WILDERNESS.

THE ARGUMENT.

As the true method of knowledge is experiment, the true
faculty of knowing must be the faculty which experiences.
This faculty I treat of.

PRINCIPLE FIRST.

That the poetic genius is the true man, and that the body
or outward form of man is derived from the poetic genius.

Likewise that the form of all things are derived from their genius, which by the ancients was called an angel and spirit and demon.

PRINCIPLE SECOND.

As all men are alike in outward form, so (and with the same infinite variety), all are alike in the poetic genius.

PRINCIPLE THIRD.

No man can think, write or speak from his heart, but he must intend truth. Thus all sects of philosophy are from the poetic genius, adapted to the weaknesses of every individual.

PRINCIPLE FOURTH.

As none by travelling over known lands can find out the unknown, so from already acquired knowledge man could not acquire more · therefore a universal poetic genius exists.

PRINCIPLE FIFTH.

The religions of all nations are derived from each nation's different reception of the poetic genius which is everywhere called the spirit of prophecy.

PRINCIPLE SIXTH.

The Jewish and Christian Testaments are an original derivation from the poetic genius. This is necessary from the confined nature of bodily sensation.

PRINCIPLE SEVENTH.

As all men are alike (though infinitely various), so all religions, and as all similars have one source.

The true man is the source, he being the poetic genius.

THERE IS NO NATURAL RELIGION.—II.

THE ARGUMENT.

MAN has no notion of moral fitness but from education Naturally, he is only a natural organ subject to sense.

I.

Man's perceptions are not bounded by organs of perception, he perceives more than sense (though ever so acute) can discover.

II.

Reason, or the ratio of all we have already known, is not the same that it shall be when we know more.

III.

From a perception of only three senses or three elements none could deduce a fourth or fifth.

IV.

None could have other than natural or organic thoughts if he had none but organic perceptions.

V.

Man's desires are limited by his perceptions ; none can desire what he has not perceived.

VI.

The desires and perceptions of man untaught by anything but organs of sense must be limited to objects of sense.

Therefore God becomes as we are, that we may be as He is.

I.

Man cannot naturally perceive but through his natural or bodily organs.

II.

Man, by his reasoning power can only compare and judge of what he has already perceived.

NOTES.

NOTES

The Poetical Sketches. Page 1.—The original edition has the following preface :—

ADVERTISEMENT.

" The following Sketches were the production of untutored youth, commenced in his twelfth, and occasionally resumed by the author till his twentieth year ; since which time, his talents having been wholly directed to the attainment of excellence in his profession, he has been deprived of the leisure requisite to such a revisal of these sheets as might have rendered them less unfit to meet the public eye.

" Conscious of the irregularities and defects found on almost every page, his friends have still believed that they possessed a poetical originality which merited some respite from oblivion. These opinions remain, however, to be now re-proved or confirmed by a less partial public."

Mr. Dante Rossetti endeavoured to make some, at any rate, of the corrections which Blake could not—or, one is inclined to suspect, would not—make, and made a number of metrical emendations in the selection of the " Sketches " given in Gilchrist's " Life and Works of William Blake." He made these with admirable judgment, but when they were made, the poems, taken as a whole, were well nigh as irregular as at the outset.

There seems no logical position between leaving the poems as they are, with all their slips of rhythm, and making alterations of a very sweeping nature, which would be out of place in a working text like the present. The present editor has accordingly simply reprinted Blake's own text, not even retaining the very small number of emendations made by Mr. W. M. Rossetti. He has, however, to economize space, left out several poems altogether, holding them mere boyish experi-

ments, with here and there some line or passage of beauty.
The poems left out are " Fair Elenor ", " Gwin, King of Nor-
way ", " Prologue to Edward the Fourth ", and four prose
poems called " Prologue to King John ", " The Couch of
Death ", " Contemplation ", and " Samson ", respectively.
" A War Song ", though scarce worthy of a place in the body of
the book, is interesting enough for quotation here.

A WAR SONG :

TO ENGLISHMEN.

Prepare, prepare the iron helm of war,
Bring forth the lots, cast in the spacious orb ;
The Angel of Fate turns them with mighty hands,
And casts them out upon the darkened earth !
     Prepare, prepare !

Prepare your hearts for Death's cold hand ! prepare
Your souls for flight, your bodies for the earth !
Prepare your arms for glorious victory !
Prepare your eyes to meet a holy God !
     Prepare, prepare !

Whose fatal scroll is that ?   Methinks 'tis mine !
Why sinks my heart, why faltereth my tongue ?
Had I three lives, I'd die in such a cause,
And rise, with ghosts, over the well-fought field.
     Prepare, prepare !

The arrows of Almighty God are drawn !
Angels of Death stand in the low'ring heavens !
Thousands of souls must seek the realms of light,
And walk together on the clouds of heaven !
     Prepare, prepare !

Soldiers, prepare !   Our cause is Heaven's cause ;
Soldiers, prepare !   Be worthy of our cause :
Prepare to meet our fathers in the sky :
Prepare, O troops that are to fall to-day !
     Prepare, prepare !

Alfred shall smile, and make his heart rejoice;
The Norman William and the learned Clerk,
And Lion-Heart, and black-browed Edward with
His loyal queen, shall rise, and welcome us !
            Prepare, prepare !

" Samson " is seen at its best in this direction to Delilah.
" Go on, fair traitress ; do thy guileful work ; ere once again
the changing moon her circuit hath performed, thou shalt
overcome and conquer him by force unconquerable, and wrest
his secret from him. Call thine alluring arts and honest-
seeming brow, the holy kiss of love and the transparent tear ;
put on fair linen that with the lily vies, purple and silver ;
neglect thy hair, to seem more lovely in thy loose attire ; put on
thy country's pride deceit ; and eyes of love decked in mild
sorrow ; and sell thy lord for gold."

The Songs of Innocence and Experience. Pages 47 to 85.—
Messrs. Dante and William Rossetti, in the second volume
of Gilchrist's Life of Blake, and in the Aldine edition of the
poems respectively, have made several grammatical and
metrical emendations. The original text is here restored.
" The Nurse's Song " and " The Little Boy Lost " are to be
found imbedded in that curious prose narrative, " The Island
of the Moon ", in slightly different form from that in " The Songs
of Innocence "; and " The Cloud and the Pebble ", " The Garden
of Love ", " The Poison Tree ", " Infant Sorrow ", " Earth's
Answer ", " London ", " The Lily ", " Nurse's Song ", " The
Tiger ", " The Human Image ", " The Sick Rose ", " The
Little Vagabond ", ",Holy Thursday ", " The Angel ", " The
Fly ", and a part of " The Chimney-Sweeper ", from the
" Songs of Experience ", are to be found in a more or less
different shape in a note-book usually spoken of by Blake's
biographers and editors as " the MS. book."

" The Songs of Innocence " and " The Song of Experience "
were latterly bound together by Blake under the title of " The
Songs of Innocence and Experience, showing the Two Con-
trary States of the Human Soul." " The MS. book " gives
the following verses with the note that they are a " motto for
the Songs of Innocence and Experience."

" The Good are attracted by men's perceptions,
　　And think not for themselves,
Till Experience teaches them to catch
　　And to cage the Fairies and Elves.

" And then the Knave begins to snarl,
　　And the Hypocrite to howl ;
And all his good friends show their private end,
　　And the Eagle is known from the Owl."

Strange lines that are clear enough to the student of Blake ₁
philosophy ; but at most a perspicuous gloom to the rest of
mankind.　The excision of " his " from the last line but one
would make them a little more intelligible.　The third and
fourth lines should be compared with " Opportunity ", page 120.
　The Tiger.　Page 74.—The MS. book contains the following
first draft for " The Tiger."　The editor has restored, where
necessary for the sense, occasional words which were crossed
out by Blake.　The poem will be found exactly as it is in the
MS. book with the crossed out words in italics, and several
alternative readings, at page 92, vol. iii., of " The Works of
William Blake."　He is at present merely anxious to give it in
the form pleasantest for the eye and the memory without the
interruption of italics and alternative readings.

THE TIGER.

Tiger, Tiger, burning bright
In the forests of the night,
What immortal hand or eye
Dare frame thy fearful symmetry ?

In what distant deeps or skies
Burned the fire within thine eyes ?
On what wings dared he aspire ?
What the hand dared seize the fire ?

And what shoulder and what art
Could twist the sinews of thy heart ?
And when thy heart began to beat,
What dread hand and what dread feet

Could filch it from the furnace deep,
And in thy hornèd ribs dare steep
In the well of sanguine woe

• • • • • • •

In what clay and in what mould
Were thine eyes of fury rolled

• • • • • • •

Where the hammer, where the chain,
In what furnace was thy brain ?
What the anvil ? what dread grasp
Dared thy deadly terrors clasp ?

Tiger, Tiger, burning bright
In the forests of the night,
What immortal hand or eye
Dare frame thy fearful symmetry ?

There is also an interesting variant upon this couplet—

" Did He smile His work to see,
    Did He who made the lamb make thee ? "

in which " laugh " is substituted for " smile."

Mr. Gilchrist and Mr. Rossetti give a version slightly different from the one found by Mr. Ellis and the present editor in the MS. book, and claim for it also MS. authority.

When Blake altered and copied out the poem for engraving he altogether omitted the unfinished fourth verse, and forgot to make the last line of the third a complete sentence. Mr. D. G. Rossetti did this for him by substituting " formed " for " and "; but Malkin, who probably had Blake's authority, prints " forged."

The Garden of Love. Page 76.—Mr. Rossetti inserts at the beginning of this poem two verses, which are here printed in " The Ideas of Good and Evil ", as a separate poem called " Thistles and Thorns." He found them in the MS. book, and forgot to notice the long line which Blake had drawn to divide them from " The Garden of Love " which followed.

The Little Vagabond. Page 76.—The MS. book gives instead
of line 9 " Such usage in heaven never do well ", " The poor
parsons with wind like a blown bladder swell."

London. Page 77.—Compare with the " blackening church,
and " marriage-hearse ", in this poem, the use of the same terms
in the following detached quatrain from the MS. book. It
is called there " An Ancient Proverb."

> Remove away that blackening church,
> Remove away that marriage-hearse,
> Remove away that man of blood,
> You'll quite remove that ancient curse.

Infant Sorrow. Page 79.—The MS. book continues this
poem as follows :—

> When I saw that rage was vain,
> And to sulk would nothing gain ;
> Turning many a trick and wile,
> I began to sooth and smile.
>
> And I soothed day after day,
> Till upon the ground I lay ;
> And I smiled night after night,
> Seeking only for delight.
>
> And I saw before me shine
> Clusters of the wandering vine ;
> And many a lovely flower and tree
> Stretched their blossoms out to me.
>
> My father, then, with holy book, (? look)
> In his hands a holy book,
> Pronouncèd curses on my head,
> And bound me in a myrtle shade.
>
> So I smote him—and his gore
> Stained the roots my myrtle bore ;
> But the time of youth is fled,
> And grey hairs are on my head.

A Cradle Song. Page 82.—This was never included by Blake in any engraved edition of " The Songs of Experience ", but it is an obvious pendant to " A Cradle Song " in " The Songs of Innocence." The editor accordingly follows Mr. Rossetti and Mr. Gilchrist in printing it here from the MS. book.

Tirzah. Page 84.—In engraved " Songs " the words " to be raised a spiritual body " are written at the end of the poem.

The Voice of the Ancient Bard. Page 85.—This poem has hitherto been printed at the end of " The Songs of Innocence." The editor, however, follows a copy of " the Songs " sold by Mrs. Blake after Blake's death to a Mr. Edwards, which was probably the last engraved, in placing it at the end of " The Songs of Experience ", where it forms a natural pendant to " The voice of the bard, who present, past, and future sees ", at the beginning.

Ideas of Good and Evil. Page 89.—The MS. book has upon its title-page the above inscription, which was possibly a first and rejected attempt towards a title for the poems afterwards called " The Songs of Innocence and Experience ", but probably a first thought for a title of " The Songs of Experience " alone, " experience " and eating the fruit of the Tree of the Know-ledge of Good and Evil being one and the same in Blake's philosophy. The first possibility is made unlikely by the fact that the MS. book contains none of " The Songs of Innocence ", which therefore probably preceded it. If this be so, it have been begun between 1789 and 1794. He kept it by him well-nigh all his life, and jotted down in it a record of all manner of wayward moods and fancies. The title " Ideas of Good and Evil " was probably soon forgotten, but, having at any rate his partial sanction, may well serve us better than such un-meaning and uncomely titles as " Later Poems " or Miscellane-ous Poems." The editor follows the example of Gilchrist's book in including under the title poems from other sources than the MS. book. The sources are letters, the engraved copy of " The Gates of Paradise ", the newly discovered " Island of the Moon ", and what the author of the note on page 85 of Gil-christ's second volume has called " another small autograph collection of different matter somewhat more fairly copied " than the MS. book. This " autograph collection " has vanished for the present, having defied all the efforts of Mr. Ellis and the present writer to discover it. It is to be hoped that it has not vanished for good and all, for the editor of the poems in Gilchrist and the editor of the Aldine edition have with a timidity which was perhaps natural in introducing for the first time an eccentric author whom the bulk of readers held to be mad, and whose meaning they themselves but partially understood, permitted themselves far too numerous transpositions, alterations, and omissions in printing from still accessible sources. The editor of the Gilchrist text, in the case of this now inaccessible " autograph collection " also,. admits to having found it " necessary " to " omit, transpose, or combine ", that he might " lessen obscurity ", but claims to have done so far less than in printing from the MS. book, and his principles were certainly adopted in the main by Mr. W. M. Rossetti in the Aldine edition. A comparison of the text given here of poems like " The Grey Monk", and poems like that which the present writer has called " Spectre and Emanation ", with the text given in either Mr. Gilchrist's or Mr. Rossetti's book, will show how much has been sacrificed in the battle with "obscurity." The student of Blake's philosophy knows well that what seems most obscure is usually most characteristic, and grudges any clearness gained at the expense of his author's meaning. He finds it even harder to forgive those cases where Mr. Rossetti did not confine himself to the right he claimed to " omit, transpose, or combine, but substituted, in the name of lucidity, words of his own for Blake's carefully selected words. These substitutions are, however, few, and probably arose from bewilderment over the strangeness of the terms, combined with the difficulty of reading the well-nigh illegible MS. Mr. Rossetti may well have refused to believe his eyes when he came, in " The Everlasting Gospel ", for instance, to " anti-Christ, creeping Jesus ", and have convinced himself that Blake meant to write " anti-Christ, aping Jesus." His sin was not so much editorial, for almost any ordinary editor would have made a mistake as human, but that sin, which he shares with a large portion of the human race, of having no feeling for mystical terms. Whatever he may have done ill in these matters is more than balanced by the great service he has done Blake in other ways. In the following selection, a few lyrics given in the Aldine or in Mr. Shepherd's edition are excluded and others included which have not appeared in either of these books. The added lyrics are, " The Pilgrim ", " A Song of Sorrow ",

and " Old English Hospitality, " from " The Island of the
Moon." The excluded poems are " La Fayette ", " To Mrs.
Butts ", " Seed Sowing ", " Idolatry ", " Long John Brown
and Little Mary Bell ", " Song by an Old Shepherd ", and
" Song by a Shepherd ", and well nigh all " the epigrams and
satirical pieces on art and artists." None of these poems,
howsoever curious and biographically interesting they be,
have poetical value anything like equal to the selections from
" The Prophetic Books ", made possible by leaving them out.
In many cases Blake gave no title to his poems, and the editor
has ventured more than once to differ from the titles chosen
by Mr. W. M. Rossetti and to substitute titles of his own.
He has never, however, done this except when the old title
seemed obviously misleading, uncharacteristic, or ungainly.

Blake's own text of " The Ideas of Good and Evil " has
been restored in the present volume in every case where the
original MS. is still accessible. The restorations are not always
to the advantage of the poem, though in some cases they cer-
tainly are ; and it is possible that the editors of the future
may prefer to make a few of those corrections which Blake
would doubtless have made had he re-copied for the press his
rough first drafts, and to keep a mid-track between the much
modified version of Messrs. Dante and William Rossetti and
the present literal text.

Auguries of Innocence. Page 90.—See note to " Proverbs."

To Mr. Butts. Page 92.—From a letter to Mr. Butts from
Felpham.

To Mrs. Flaxman. Page 95.—From a letter to Flaxman
from Felpham.

Proverbs. Page 96.—This is one of the poems taken from
that other " small autograph collection " mentioned in Gil-
christ. Mr. Herne Shepherd gives in " Blake's Poems and
Songs of Innocence " (Pickering & Chatto) a version different
in the order of the verses, and in having several grammatical
and one or two obvious metrical slips, not present in the version
given by Mr. Dante Rossetti in Gilchrist's book. Even if
Mr. Shepherd gave the text with accuracy, it is impossible
to say in the absence of the manuscript how far he read Blake's
intentions correctly. The poem is a series of magnificent
proverbs and epigrams, rather than a poem with middle, be-
ginning, and end, and Blake in all likelihood set these proverbs

and epigrams down in order of composition, and not in order
of thought and subject. The manuscript was never corrected
for the press, and may have been little more than a series of
notes to help his own memory. Mr. D. G. Rossetti may there-
fore, in putting the lines in order of thought and subject, have
gone really nearer to Blake's own intention than Mr. Herne
Shepherd in printing them in the order of the manuscript.
One is the more ready to believe this, because the poem as
arranged by Mr. Rossetti was incomparably finer than Mr.
Shepherd's version. The writer has, therefore, adopted Mr.
Rossetti's version. Mr. Rossetti has also left out several
couplets given by Shepherd. The writer at first thought of
restoring these, but on second thought prints them here, as
they would assuredly mar with their clumsy rhythm and loose
structure the magnificent sweetness and power of one of the
greatest of all Blake's poems.

The couplet—

> " Every tear in every eye
> Becomes a babe in eternity "—

was continued as follows—

> " This is caught by females aright,
> And return'd to its own delight."

a little further down came the lines—

> " The babe that weeps the rod beneath,
> Writes revenge in realms of death ; "

and towards the end of the poem—

> " To be in a passion you good may do,
> But no good if a passion is in you."

In one matter, however, the editor has differed both from
the version of Mr. Herne Shepherd and Mr. Gilchrist. He
is entirely convinced that the title " Auguries of Innocence ",
refers only to the first four lines of this version. Blake was
most exact in the use of terms, and would never have called
either " The harlot's cry from the street ", or " The whore
and gambler by the state licensed ", or " The questioner who
sits so sly ", or " The wanton boy who kills the fly ", or well
nigh any of the things mentioned in this poem, " Auguries of
Innocence."

He did, upon the other hand, hold that " Innocence " or the state of youthful poetic imagination was none other than to " see a world in a grain of sand " and " a heaven in a wild flower." Neither Mr. Rossetti nor Mr. Shepherd believed Blake to use words with philosophical precision, but held him a vague dreamer carried away by his imagination, and may well have never given two thoughts to anything except the imaginative charm of the title. We have already seen how Mr. W. M. Rossetti tacked on to " The Garden of Love " two verses which Blake had clearly marked off as a separate poem. In this case, too, there was probably a line drawn between the first quatrain and the rest of the poem, and even if there were not, the internal evidence is itself conclusive. The editor has, therefore, printed the " Auguries of Innocence " as a poem by itself, and called the lines thus separated from them " Proverbs ", as that is a title used by Blake in " The Marriage of Heaven and Hell " for short gnomic sayings of the kind.

In a Myrtle Shade. Page 103.—The poem printed is the final version chosen by Blake, but the MS. book contains two other versions which are not uninteresting. The first should be compared with the poem quoted in the notes to " Infant Sorrow." It is as follows :—

> To a lovely myrtle bound,
> Blossoms showering all around
>
> O how weak and weary I
> Underneath my myrtle lie,
> Like to dung upon the ground,
> Underneath my myrtle bound.
>
> Why should I be bound to thee,
> O my lovely myrtle tree ?
> Love, free love, cannot be bound
> To any tree that grows on ground.
>
> Oft my myrtle sighed in vain,
> To behold my heavy chain ;
> Oft my father saw us sigh,
> And laughed at our simplicity.

So I smote him, and his gore
Stained the roots my myrtle bore ;
But the time of youth is fled,
And grey hairs are on my head.

The second version is :—

TO MY MYRTLE.

Why should I be bound to thee,
O my lovely myrtle tree ?
Love, free love, cannot be bound
To any tree that grows on ground.
To a lovely myrtle bound,
Blossom showering all around,
Underneath my myrtle bound,
O how weak and weary I
Underneath my myrtle lie.

There is written beside these versions in pencil a stanza,
now almost illegible, of which the following words can be made
out :—

Deceit to seeming   *   *   *
*   *   *   *   refined
To everything but interest blind,
And   *   *   *   fetters every mind,
And forges fetters of the mind.

We give this fragment because it was the origin of a stanza
interpolated in Gilchrist's book in the middle of the poem 1
call " Freedom and Captivity." It was no doubt more legible
than at present when Mr. D. G. Rossetti copied it out, and the
word that looks more like " seeming " may perhaps be really
" secrecy." His reading, too, of the lines, which are now
quite illegible, is probably to be trusted. His version is as
follows :—

" Deceit to secrecy inclined
Moves, lawful, courteous and refined,
To everything but interest blind,
And forges fetters for the mind."

The Two Thrones. Page 104.—This poem, which is given no title by Blake, is called "Mammon," and is much edited in Mr. W. M. Rossetti's edition. It is here given exactly as in the MS. book.

The Two Kinds of Riches. Page 105.—The MS. book gives no title.

The Grey Monk. Page 109.—This poem was originally intended, as the MS. book shows, to have been the latter half of a poem of fourteen stanzas, which began with the line, " I saw a monk of Constantine." Blake changed this first line into " I saw a monk of Charlemagne ", made a few other alterations here and there, and divided the poem into two parts. To the first half of four stanzas he added three stanzas, and printed it in the preface to chap. iii. of " Jerusalem " (see page 201). The second half he left without change or addition. The arrangement of the verses in the Aldine edition is quite arbitrary. Mr. Rossetti has made the second stanza in Blake's MS. the third in his version, and the third the fourth, and the fourth the fifth, and the fifth the seventh, and the seventh the ninth, and left out Blake's own ninth stanza altogether. He has also imported a stanza from " The Monk of Charlemagne ", and made it the second stanza. Mr. Rossetti made no secret of his transposition and suppression, so that no great blame attaches to him in this matter. He had to introduce Blake to an unwilling generation, and thought it best to lop off many an obtrusive knot and branch.

The Everlasting Gospel. Page 110.—Mr. Rossetti has by a slip of the pen claimed to give this poem " in full " (see Aldine edition, page 144), and has not only not done so, but has given passages out of the order intended by Blake, and printed words here and there which are not in Blake at all. The poem is not given in full in the present book ; for it is not possible to do so without many repetitions, for Blake never made a final text. The MS. book contains three different versions of a large portion of the poem, and it is not possible to keep wholly to any one of these without sacrificing many fine passages. Blake left, however, pretty clear directions for a great part of the text-making, and these directions were ignored by Mr. Rossetti. The short fragment which begins the poem both in the present and in the Aldine text was probably intended to be a private dedication apparently to Stothard, and not a part of the poem at all. The present editor follows Mr. Rossetti in leaving out two ungainly lines about the length of Stothard's nose and the shortness of Blake's (see " Works of William Blake", vol. ii, page 44). Had Blake ever printed the dedication he also would doubtless have suppressed these lines. The poem was intended by him to begin with the lines which open " Was Jesus humble, or did He give any proofs of humility ? " for he has written the title above them. Mr. Rossetti puts these lines almost at the very end. There are two other versions of the first part of the poem, and passages are here added from one of these versions. There still remain two fragments, the one is marked by Blake as containing " 94 lines ", though later additions slightly increased its length, and the other contains 48 lines, and is printed on a slip of paper at the end of the book. There is a mark at the foot of the " 94 line " fragment signifying that it is to follow the lines over which Blake had written the title. It begins, " Was Jesus chaste ", and ends, " For dust and clay is the serpent's meat, That never was meant for man to eat." The 48 line fragment begins, " Was Jesus born of a virgin pure ", and ends, " God's righteous law that lost its prey." There still remains a couplet, " I am sure this Jesus will not do Either for Christian or for Jew." Blake marks it to follow the " 94 lines ", but this mark may have been made before the writing of the lines beginning " Was Jesus born of a virgin pure ", for certainly its place is at the end of all. There are also a few fragmentary lines here and there of whose place no indication is given. All the fragments are given separately in " The Works of William Blake."

To Nobodady. Page 120.—Printed by Mr. Rossetti without Blake's quaint title. In a later version Blake changed the last line to " Gains females' loud applause."

Cupid. Page 122.—The MS. book gives the following fifth stanza :—

> 'Twas the Greeks' love of war
> Turned Cupid into a boy,
> And woman into a statue of stone ;
> Away flew every joy.

Spectre and Emanation. Page 129.—Mr. Dante Rossetti read this as primarily a love poem, and was led by this mistake into calling it "Broken Love." Blake gives no title, but "Spectre and Emanation" is his technical expression for reason and emotion, active and passive, masculine and feminine, past and future, body and soul, and all the other duads of his complex system. Both Mr. Dante Gabriel Rossetti in Gilchrist's Life of Blake, and Mr. W. M. Rossetti in the Aldine, adopt an arrangement of the verses not to be found in the MS. book.

The verses in the text are those numbered by Blake as part of the poem. There are, however, certain other verses which were apparently rejected by him. They are as follows:—

> O'er my sins thou dost sit and moan,
> Hast thou no sins of thine own ?
> O'er my sins thou dost sit and weep,
> And lull thy own sins fast asleep.
>
> What transgressions I commit
> Are for thy transgression fit :
> They thy harlots, thou their slave ;
> And thy bed becomes their grave.
>
> Poor, pale, pitiable form
> That I follow in a storm !
> Iron tears and groans of lead
> Bind around my aching head.

Los the Terrible. Page 136.—This extract from a letter to Mr. Butts, dated November, 1802, and described as having been "composed above a twelve month ago, while walking from Felpham to Levant, to meet my sister", has no title in the original. "Los the Terrible" describes the subject of the poem, which is Los in his malevolent rather than in his more usual benevolent aspect.

Tiriel. Page 147.—The style of the poem, which resembles rather that of "The Mental Traveller" than the more vehement and broken style of the later prophetic poems, makes it clear that "Tiriel" belongs to an earlier period than any other of the prophetic books. It was probably followed by "The Ghost of Abel!" Mr. Rossetti says : "the handwriting appears to me to belong to no late period of his life. This character of handwriting prevails up to near the close of the poem. With the words (in section 8), " I am Tiriel, King of the West ", a new and less precise kind of handwriting begins ; clearly indicating, I think, that Blake, after an interval of some years, took up the poem and finished it, perhaps in much more summary fashion than he at first intended." The style of the later lines seems to the present writer to be much later than the style of the rest of the poem. It is more directly mystical, more of a direct appeal from the soul of Blake to the soul of the reader, and much more wholly dependent upon mystical knowledge for its interest. The rest of the poem has a certain interest and meaning as a story, but this latter page is as purely mystical as " Europe ", or " America ", or " Jerusalem." It is symbolical rather than allegorical.

Thel. Page 169.—This poem was engraved in 1789. The engraved copy begins " The daughters of Mne Seraphim ", Blake having apparently thought of writing " The daughters of Mnetha ", Mnetha being the name given in his system to the Mother of All. The letters " Mne " are scratched out in the Bodleian copy, and it is possible that Blake got into the habit of reading " Mne " as " the ", and of so giving the rhythm the syllable it requires.

The Marriage of Heaven and Hell. Page 176.—This poem was engraved in 1790, and is a reply to the then recently trans‧lated " Heaven and Hell " of Swedenborg

Visions of the Daughters of Albion. Page 194.—This poem was engraved in 1793, and is not only one of the most beautiful but one of the most subtle and difficult of " the prophetic books."

Ahania. Page 207.—This poem was engraved in 1795 There is a copy, the only one extant, of Blake's edition, in the library of Lord Houghton.

Vala. Page 218.—This poem was never engraved by Blake, It was probably written during the last three or four years of the century. The manuscript was given by Blake to his friend Linnell, the landscape painter, but at what date is not now known. The extracts given are from the second and eighth books respectively.

Jerusalem. Page 221.—it is dated 1804, but Blake was probably at work upon it both before and after that date.

Milton. Page 233.—Also dated 1804, but like " Jerusalem ", probably not finished until a later date. It was originally intended to run to twelve books, but Blake finished it in two.

On his Picture of the Canterbury Pilgrims. Page 239.—From the Descriptive Catalogue which was published in 1809.

Identity. Page 250.—From a number of disordered notes in the MS. book which seem to have been intended as an introduction to his description of his picture of "The Last Judgment."

Minute Knowledge. Page 251.—From Blake's sequel to his description of the picture of "The Last Judgment."

The Nature of a Last Judgment. Page 251.—From the same source with the last.

Why Men enter Heaven. Page 252. From the same source with the last.

Learning without Imagination. Page 253.—From the description, in the Descriptive Catalogue, of the picture of "A Spirit vaulting from a Cloud."

Form and Substance are One. Page 253.—From the scraps of a "Public Address" which are scattered about the MS. book, and which were printed by Gilchrist in a somewhat arbitrary order.

Good and Evil.—Page 253. From the sequel to his description of the picture of "The Last Judgment."

The Clearness of Vision. Page 254.—From the description in the Descriptive Catalogue, of his picture "The Bard from Gray."

Outline in Art and Life. Page 254.—From the description, in the Descriptive Catalogue, of "Ruth—a Drawing."

The Tree of Good and Evil. Page 255. From the sequel to his description of the picture of "The Last Judgment." It is omitted in Gilchrist perhaps because Blake himself drew a line through it. It was probably objected to by Blake simply because it added to the obscurity, without greatly helping the argument, of his " sequel", and not because he disapproved of it in itself, for it states more shortly and explicitly than elsewhere a fundamental conception of his.

There is no Natural Religion, I, II. Pages 255, 256.—From the engraved, but undated, and illustrated tractates.

THE END.